How To
Write
Your Own
Life Story

How To Write Your Own Life Story

The Classic Guide for the Nonprofessional Writer

FOURTH EDITION

Lois Daniel

CHICAGO
REVIEW
PRESS

Library of Congress Cataloging-in-Publication Data

Daniel, Lois.
    How to write your own life story: the classic guide for the
non-professional writer / Lois Daniel. — 4th ed., rev. and expanded.
        p.   cm.
    Includes bibliographical references.
    ISBN 1-55652-318-1 (paper)
    1. Autobiography   I. Title.
CT25.D36   1997
808'.06692—dc21   96-52438
                                                                       CIP

"Breakfast on the Beach" is reprinted here with permission from
Unity School of Christianity, Unity Village, MO 64065.
The Willa Cather quote (page 155, in chapter 22) is taken from Phyllis C. Robinson,
Willa, The Life of Willa Cather (New York: Doubleday & Co., 1983), p. 20.

© 1980, 1985, 1991, 1997 Lois Daniel
All rights reserved
Fourth edition
Published by Chicago Review Press, Incorporated
814 North Franklin Street
Chicago, Illinois 60610
Printed in the United States of America
ISBN 1-55652-318-1
5 4

To Carol Dechant,
whose encouragement has been so much a part of
this book that she almost deserves a byline.

Contents

Introduction

The idea for this book came out of a failure. Several years ago I was teaching a creative writing class at Longview College in Lee's Summit, Missouri. In many ways the class was a complete success. The students were enthusiastic, seldom missed a session, and two even sold articles to magazines before the semester ended. However, I felt that I completely failed one student—a seventy-five-year-old woman.

When I asked each student to state his or her reason for joining the class, this lady's reason was that her children had been begging her to write the story of her life. "I don't know how to do it," she said, "and I thought you might be able to help me."

Frankly, I had no idea how to help her. The course was designed to help students who wished to become professional writers turn their article and story ideas into salable manuscripts. I hadn't the faintest idea how to help an inexperienced writer write the story of her life. My suggestions, which were being received enthusiastically by the other students, were of no value whatsoever to this woman, and she finally dropped out of the class. I counted her leaving as a definite failure on my part, but at that time I didn't know what to do about it.

I felt especially bad since I knew how much my family and I valued a story that my mother (with much urging from us) had written about an incident in her life. It was the story of a trip she made in a covered wagon from Minnesota to Missouri when she was five years old. We love the story as a family history and also as an interesting, detailed account of an actual covered wagon trip. However, the story was of special value to me for a very personal reason.

My parents were well along in years when I was born. This made me a second generation in my own family and my mother was distant from me in both years and personality. I viewed her as a very old, very strong, very domineering woman. When I read her story, which is filled with funny and sometimes heartbreaking incidents from her childhood, she, for the first time, seemed to me to be a vulnerable human being. I was grateful to have this new view of her even though it came late in our relationship.

As I thought about how I valued my mother's story I wanted very much to develop a course to help adult students write about their lives. I wanted to help them produce material that would be precious to their families—on whatever level was appropriate for each family. Perhaps in addition to serving as an historic link for past, present, and future generations, some of the stories might even help resolve old conflicts and promote understanding among family members.

Something else that gave me a sense of urgency about helping adults write their memoirs is the fact that although my father had been dead for nearly thirty years I had recently had a great longing to know something about him as a young man. I know that soon after he graduated from high school he roamed over the western states for two or three years before marrying my mother and settling down to become the most dependable and affectionate of family men.

I remember when I was a child, and later when I was in my teens, hearing my father tell about his youthful experiences—hopping freight cars, doing menial work on ranches, winding up penniless in drab, ugly western towns. I was always terribly embarrassed when he told these tales outside the family because I thought they made him sound like a ne'er-do-well. I scolded him for telling his stories because I didn't want people to think my father had been a bum. I realize now that he was not a bum at all but an interesting and adventurous young man, and I should have drunk in every word he uttered about his travels. Some years ago I took a history course entitled "Myths and Realities of the Old West." The course covered the West up until 1900. Suddenly, it dawned on me that it was in the late 1890s that my father was there. He had seen and been part of the last days of what we call the Old West and I had begged him not to talk about it!

I recall three of his western adventures, and I have recounted them elsewhere in this book, not with embarrassment but with pride. However, the real story of the youth of this man who I loved wholeheartedly and who showered me with love and made innumerable sacrifices for me is lost to me forever. I feel that this loss of continuity in the generations of our families is a tragic flaw in our society. Of course, each generation must find its own way, but must each generation be rootless, denied knowledge of its heritage? I hope not.

I read my mother's story many times as I tried to devise a method of helping students find an easy, fun, and stimulating way of writing about the events of their lives. Suddenly one evening as I was rereading the story I thought, "I know what the key is! We didn't ask mother to write the story of her *entire* life. That would have seemed like an overwhelming task, which she probably would never have attempted. We only asked her to write about her trip from Minnesota."

I realized that the way to make autobiographical writing easy was to help students divide their lives into small and manageable segments. Next I would devise a system of memory association exercises which would help them recall long-forgotten but important incidents. With these ideas as a beginning, I started developing plans for a class designed exclusively for inexperienced writers who wanted to write the story of their lives for themselves and their families.

I have taught the course successfully numerous times, and students have recalled wonderful—often forgotten—experiences and been able to put them on paper. They have reported how thrilled their children are to have the stories. One woman said, "My children pester me constantly to know when 'the story' will be finished. We haven't spent as much time talking together in years as we have since I began my writing."

I developed the course with the idea of teaching it to older, mostly retired persons. However, when I was forming my second class a woman in her early forties asked rather timidly, "Does a person have to be old to come to your class?" I naturally said "no," and she became an enthusiastic student. (In fact, she is the little Georgian girl whose story is included in this book's chapter on religion.)

It still did not occur to me, however, that young people in their twenties and thirties might be interested in the course. If I had thought about them at all, I suppose I would have thought they would be busy going to school, getting started in jobs, getting married, raising young families, and more. Also, I probably would have judged them by myself at their age and assumed that they would have been so caught up in thinking about their present and future that they would have no interest in writing about their past.

Occasionally, though, I mentioned my classes in casual conversation with young friends and I was astounded to see their immediate interest in the subject. Time after time, I heard even very young people say longingly, "Oh, there is so much I have wanted to write about my life, but I don't know how." Almost before I knew it, I was holding an autobiographical workshop for young people.

Among these young students I have found stories just as exciting and just as inspiring as those written by older persons. I have met a young woman in her early thirties who grew up as part of a Mafia family and who had to grapple with the conflict of her deep love for her uncle and her adult realization of who and what this man actually was. I have met a young woman who, in the aftermath of a devastating divorce, developed a pattern for survival which could be an inspiration for both young and old.

As I have worked with these young students I have come to believe that time has brought us to a point where young people have a great hunger for discovering enduring values. I think their interest in writing about their own lives, both past and present, is an attempt to partially assuage that hunger.

You note I said writing about their past *and present*. Several young students have asked, "Will it be all right if I write about the job I have right now?" One young woman who is a single parent asked, "Would it be okay for me to write about what it's like for a mother to raise a son alone?" This interest in writing about the present opened up a whole new idea to me. What if people would start writing about their lives as they go along? That's what people in the past did. If it hadn't been for the fact that keeping diaries was the custom in the early days of our country much, perhaps most, of our history would have been lost forever.

Finally, after working with people of all ages, I knew that my book would have to be for everyone. I hoped it would help older persons who have more time, have lived longer lives, and have greater perspective write about times which are slipping rapidly from our view. For the young I dared to hope that it might cause at least a few to make writing about their lives as they lived them a lifelong hobby.

I have outlined my method of autobiographical writing in this book. It is a method that can be used not only by a class but also by an individual writing alone at home. The book has been out in various editions and revisions for sixteen years, and interest in it continues. The warm reception accorded it has been very gratifying. Like all writers I love having people like what I write. However, what has pleased me most is the fact that the book has seemed to meet a very real need. Interest in it confirms what I have already sensed to be true, that thousands of Americans hunger for information about their families.

Evidence of this hunger has been brought to my attention in many interesting ways. I have been invited to talk about the book in various parts of the country and always after my speeches people come up to me and want to buy at least one and often several books. At a Rotary Club luncheon a man, who was not atypical, said, "I want four books, one for my parents, one for my grandparents, and one for each of my two aunts. I'm hoping they'll all write something." Another man wanted a book for himself and his wife, one for his parents, and one for his wife's parents. I believe these people already had a yearning to know something about their families before they heard me speak. I simply offered a way to help satisfy that yearning.

I have received dozens of letters from people in forty-two states and to my amazement people in twenty-six states have called Kansas City directory assistance, gotten my telephone number, and called me. Some want to ask a question about autobiographical writing, some want to know whether I will be speaking anywhere near their community, others have an unusual story they think I would like to hear. Often, though, they have called just to chat about their writing. These calls and letters please me because I hoped the book would reach people on a very personal level and that readers would feel as if we were working on their writing project together.

I have also received calls from high school and college teachers who said they were using the book in their classes. One college professor told me he felt it is no longer just desirable for young people to know something about the history of their country and their families; he thinks it has become a critical need. This man, who has taught for many years, said he and his colleagues are facing a new challenge with today's students. "It's hard to know how to reach them," he said. "They don't seem to be connected to anything. They have no idea who they are or where they come from. They've grown up with the futuristic orientation of science fiction, had a steady diet of computer games, and watched an endless procession of television shows where everything is solved in an hour or half hour."

I am especially pleased when people tell me ways the book has inspired their own creativity. When it first came out, the publisher arranged radio and television interviews for me in several cities. A young woman who interviewed me on a Chicago radio station said, "As soon as I read your book I sent twelve stamped, self-addressed envelopes to six members of my family who are scattered around the country and told them I expected a story from them every month for a year. I promised that if they sent their stories I would edit them, photocopy them, and put them all in a book and send everyone a copy."

Another young woman comes from a large family that gathers from several states at Christmas. After reading the book, she sent a mimeographed letter to all members of her family asking them to write a story about their lives to be read around the Christmas tree. The family has been doing this now for several years.

I have seen a great deal of evidence that many people not only want to know about their families but also have a strong desire to write their own stories. A year or so after the book came out I received a letter from Aleon DeVore in Englewood, Colorado, who was coordinator for the Rocky Mountain Writers Guild's Senior Writing Competition. This was a nationwide contest which invited people sixty years old and older to write a story about an incident in their lives. The contest committee had hoped for perhaps a thousand entries but received nearly six thousand from all fifty states and eleven foreign countries.

Aleon had read my book and asked whether I would be a judge in the contest's finals. I agreed and forty-five wonderful stories wound up on my coffee table. You can imagine the fun I had reading them. More important, you can imagine the fun the thousands of contestants had writing them. Eight of these stories are included in this edition of the book. Each one is followed by an asterisk to identify it as a contest entry.

I could easily answer in the affirmative when my publisher asked whether I had new material that would justify bringing out a second edition of this book. I had taught the course many times since this book was introduced and had new stories to share, as well as some new writing tips. Then there was a third edition that came out in 1991 and here, now, is the fourth edition of *How to Write Your Own Life Story*.

I am very glad the book is going to continue to be available, because I am more convinced than ever that there is a great need for us to cease discarding our memories as unimportant. I feel we must take some responsibility for meeting the need described by the college professor who said his students do not seem to be connected to anything. We can help today's young people as well as future generations know where they came from, which may help them discover who they are. The story of your life will be a gift to your family that only you can give.

Lois Daniel
July, 1996
Kansas City, Missouri

Setting Up Your Memory Bank

Y ou will need two loose-leaf notebooks for writing your story. One is the book you will write in. This one will need lined paper if you are going to write by hand or plain paper if you use a type-writer or a computer. If you write by hand, write only on every second or third line so you will be able to add words and thoughts, make corrections, and more. If you type, always double space for the same reason.

The other notebook, which should definitely have lined paper, is your memory bank, into which you will deposit facts about your past as they come to mind—just a few words to keep the thought from getting away is all you need to put down. You will find that these facts will gather "interest" just like a savings account. As you read them over again and again and begin to write your story, one memory will spark another and multiply itself many times. Make a note of each of these new memories and soon you will have a wealth of material from which to write your story.

As you begin to work, you will use the first fifty-one pages of your memory bank notebook, one for each assignment. You may use more later but this will get you started. In the upper right-hand corner of each page, using a red pencil, copy from your book the name of each assignment (see Assignments, p. 243), one assignment to a page. For example, your first page will be (1–Birth), your second (2–Toys), and so on. Make a page for each assignment in the book right in the beginning—don't wait until you come to each assignment in the book—because if the pages are all ready you will be more likely to jot down and save ideas as they come to you.

Ground Rules

*I*n her beautiful and simply written autobiography, *Grandma Moses: My Life's Story*, Anna Mary Moses tells us exactly how she wrote the story of her life. She says, "I have written my life in small sketches, a little today, a little yesterday, as I have thought of it, as I remember all the things from childhood on through the years, good ones, and unpleasant ones, that is how they come out and that is how we have to take them."

One could scarcely find a better formula for writing one's life story, and I hope you will resolve to begin to write about your life in small sketches, a little today, a little tomorrow, as you remember all of the things from your childhood and through the years, both the good things and the unpleasant things. This book is designed to help you do exactly that.

Here are a few ground rules that I would like for you to apply as you work on this exciting project:

1. **Don't worry about how it sounds.** Don't work for style. Just write whatever comes into your head as if you were writing a

letter to your closest friend. Many beginning students worry so much about achieving a certain style in their writing that they can't get beyond the first paragraph. Don't waste a minute in this manner. There will be plenty of time later if you want to revise. (There is a chapter on revision later in the book.) Even many professional writers write their first drafts without any thought as to how their work sounds. They just want to get their story down on paper.

2. **Be yourself.** Write the way you talk. Don't be embarrassed if you know that your grammar is faulty. This is your story and it should sound like you. The way you have talked all of your life is the way you should write and the way that will best reflect you. One of the most delightful autobiographies I have ever read is *Anything Can Happen* by George Papashvily, an immigrant from Georgia, formerly part of the Soviet Union. It is written in badly garbled English, but that is part of its charm. Here is an example of Papashvily's writing in which he tells about being apprenticed to a swordmaker when he was 10 years old:

Work 14 hours in every day and the master's wife had a pleasure to wash, always to wash. In suds and out of, rubbing and scrubbing, even the walls and window and street before the door knew her brush and mop. And for all this I had the duty in my spare time to carry buckets of water from the well. Coupla days in the house and a person could enjoy to be dirty rest of his life.

In spite of the language handicap (which actually added charm to his book and thus proved to be more an asset than a handicap), Papashvily managed to write a touching and often hilariously funny book.

One of my students, who grew up in the Ozarks, wrote about a "poke" full of potatoes. Several of the members of the class didn't know what a poke was, and she had to explain that it was a sack. She started to substitute "sack" for "poke" when she realized that the other students didn't understand what she was talking about. However, we all insisted that she leave it exactly as she had written it. The word poke added a valuable regional flavor to her story.

3. **Be honest.** Don't write about things as you wish they had been. Write about them the way they actually were. Take time to think through each incident and be sure you are telling it exactly as it happened, trimming away anything you may have added mentally through the years.

   All good writing is an excursion into honesty. We rush madly along through life, often acting or reacting in a given situation without thinking much about how we really feel about it. When we write about our lives, we must take time to analyze our thoughts, our feelings, and our actions. If you have never written before, you will find this sort of analysis a rewarding experience. You will start to write something and a little voice inside you will say, "Just a minute, is that the way it really happened?" or "What did you really think about that—what do you think about that now?" When this voice speaks to you, take time to listen to it and then heed it. You may find you will meet someone with whom you have had little time to get acquainted—yourself! (Of course, as you begin to unlock your closet of memories some skeletons that you just don't want to write about may tumble out. If so, it's your choice whether to include them in your story. Just be sure that everything you do write is as honest as you can make it.)

4. **Don't let your story be just a sterile recital of events.** Write about your feelings and opinions. Talk about your relationships with the people in your family, the people you worked with, went to school with, and so on. How did you feel about them?

5. **Whenever possible, relate things that happened in the distant past to things that have happened in the present or recent past.** This isn't always possible, but when it is, it will greatly enrich your story. I will give an example of relating distant and recent past events in Assignment Two and later in the chapter on revision.

6. **Read some books that other people have written about their lives.** There is a list of recommended autobiographies in the back of this book. Of course there are thousands of others, but these are books that I have read or that my students have read and recommend. You will enjoy reading them and they will remind you of things you will want to write about. Incidentally, I heartily recommend that as soon as possible you go to the library and get a copy of Grandma Moses' book. It is short and simply written and you can read it very quickly. I believe it will start you thinking about your own past and fill you with enthusiasm for your writing.

7. **Remember to include humor.** Your life wasn't all serious so don't let your descendants think it was. Tell them about some of the things that made you laugh when they happened and about others that didn't seem funny at the time but at which you were able to laugh in retrospect.

8. **Share a little wisdom with your descendants.** What sustained you through life's rough spots? The people who read your story are bound to have difficult times and it may help them to know you had problems and survived. But don't yield to the temptation to lecture them!

9. **Describe the scenes in which the events you recount took place.** Did the kitchen have a wood stove? A pump or water bucket? Kerosene lamps? Rag rugs?

10. **Reread this list of ground rules often as you are writing.**

THREE

Working On Your Assignments

You will note that the assignments are not necessarily in chrono-logical order. You can arrange them chronologically when you put your story together if you want to. However, sometimes flash-backs make a story more interesting and so does occasionally reaching forward to tie the past to the present. You may want to arrange some of your stories with these thoughts in mind. There are many ar-rangement possibilities. We will cover these in the chapter on revision and pulling it all together.

You may not want to work on the assignments in the order that they are presented in this book. That's fine. Work on them as memo-ries come to you and as you are able to gather necessary information. The main thing is to start writing and keep writing. If you hit a snag because you need to write to a relative to fill in some facts or need to go to the library to confirm dates, make a note on the appropriate assignment page in your memory bank. Jot down the information you need and the steps you have taken or intend to take to get it and go on to something else in the meantime. I have known of several potentially valuable personal histories that have floundered because the writer felt compelled to write in chronological order and was stumped for a few facts.

When you finish writing an assignment, take it out of your writing notebook and put it behind the appropriate page in your memory bank notebook. You can add more to any assignment later if you think of more you want to say. Since the pages are all loose-leaf it will be easy to slip additions in with the proper story.

Of course, you won't be working with a class, but working with this book will be very much like attending one of my classes. In class I make an assignment of one of the topics listed in the book. Students then go home and write their stories based on the subject assigned. The next week they read their stories aloud. I make no attempt to correct the written assignments unless a student asks for help, and there are no lectures on writing techniques. All we want to do is to trigger as many of the student's memories as possible and get them down on paper.

Listening to others read their assignments aloud starts students' memory association processes working. One person's story will remind someone else of something he or she wants to write. For example, one man wrote that his father used to whittle a lot in the evening. This reminded another student that her father used to carve tops out of wooden spools. "Dad would get lots of tops spinning at one time in one of mother's big flat cake pans," she said. "We kids all used to lie on our stomachs on the floor around the pan in front of the kitchen stove and see how many tops he could have spinning at one time before some of them began to run down. I remember he got twenty-one going once. I don't remember whether he ever topped that or not, but it used to be a real family game to play with those tops."

This book will provide the same kind of memory association exercises for you. In each assignment I have not only given suggestions for how to go about working on it, I have also included one or more sample life history stories on the subject of the assignment. Reading these stories will remind you of things you want to write about, give you ideas of ways to present your stories, and generally inspire you.

Perhaps you won't want to do some of the assignments. That is up to you, but put the pages in your memory bank anyway. As you work through the various assignments you may remember some things you have forgotten and you might find you want to do the assignment after all.

Perhaps you will think of some assignments that are especially applicable to your life. If so, make up a special page for each of these. For example, in *Anything Can Happen* George Papashvily devotes an entire chapter to his almost desperate search in the United States for someone who could speak Georgian. He spoke enough English to get along in his everyday life and enough Russian and Turkish to speak with a few other immigrants, but he had a terrible hunger to hear and speak his own language. The chapter about his two-year search for one of his countrymen is a fascinating addition to his book. You may have a special subject like this that will add something unique to your story. If so, by all means make a memory page for it and then write it.

One of the first things beginning journalism students are taught is that every news story must answer the following questions for the reader: Who? What? Why? How? Where? and When? You should keep these words in mind as you write your story. Down the left-hand side of each assignment sheet in your memory bank (using your red pencil again so they will stand out) write these six words, leaving several lines between each word for notes. Make notes on the memory sheet under the appropriate heading as they occur to you, and when you actually do your writing be sure that all or most of these six questions are answered.

So, now let's begin—the first assignment is your birth page.

Birth

First, we have to put a few vital statistics into your memory bank on your birth page. I will use the birth information of one of my students as a sample.

Who: Doris Pettit

What: A girl

Where: At Fort Leavenworth, Kansas

When: May 15, 1893

Why: A superficial answer to this question would be that she was born there because her father, an army officer, was stationed there. However, only her entire life story will actually tell why she was born.

How: Delivered by a Dr. Miller

Parents: Garver and Ellen Pettit—Married September 18, 1882.

Now we come to a fascinating part of making up your birth page. Do you know what kind of world you were born into? Not the kind of a world you first remember, but the kind into which you were actually born? Of twenty students in my last class—all relatively well educated—only nine knew for sure who was president of the United States when they were born. Most were quite chagrined to discover their lack of this knowledge, but that's how it was.

An exciting way to discover the world into which you were born is to read a newspaper published the day you were born. If you live in a large city, your public library probably has microfilms of old newspapers. (The Kansas City, Missouri Public Library, for example, has microfilms of the *Kansas City Star* as far back as 1881.) Call your library, tell them the date of the paper you need, and ask whether they have it. If they do, plan to spend at least half a day reading a microfilm of the paper. It is an engrossing experience. You'll love the advertisements!

One thing I discovered was that the clothes I first remember seeing bore no resemblance to the clothes that people were wearing at the time I was born. There was a drastic style change between my birth and my earliest memory.

Make notes in your memory bank of all important information about what was going on on your birth date. Later, use the information to write a story about what was happening on that date. You might get some photocopies made of interesting pictures, stories, and advertisements and paste them in your finished book.

If there were any interesting or unusual circumstances surrounding your birth be sure to include them. One woman, for example, says that when she was fifty-six years old she discovered she had been born "nowhere," and in writing about her birth she reminds us of how very young our country is:

I was born on October 14, 1905, in Santa Fe, New Mexico, daughter of Mansel Thomas and Lottie Bell (Gould) Williams. I was a very small "blue" baby and the doctor gave me little chance of surviving. My parents had selected the name Lillian, if the baby were a girl, but they had not decided on a middle name. In our church it is the practice to have babies blessed instead of baptized. My mother and father wanted me blessed before I died but were so distraught about my dying that they could not give even a thought to a second name for me. My grandfather, Mortimore Burrows Williams, was living with us for a short time, and he had been reading a poem which was signed "Carabel." He said to my parents, "Why not Carabel for a middle name?" They agreed.

Grandpa was an elder in the church and was authorized to bless babies so he blessed me sometime during the night. I have carried the name Lillian Carabel for more than seventy-three years. I have never liked my middle name and my mother has admitted that she didn't care much for it either. "But," she said to me on one occasion, "I thought you were only going to have to live with it for a few hours!"

We moved to Missouri before I was a year old. I had always heard that New Mexico was not yet a state when I was born but I had never thought much about it until I was fifty-six years old and planning a trip to Europe. I needed a birth certificate in order to get a passport but I discovered that the New Mexico territorial government had kept no vital statistics and there was no record of my birth. Suddenly, I felt as if I had been born "nowhere!" It took me nearly four months to assemble all of the information New Mexico required in order to acknowledge my birth. As I write this in 1979 I can't help thinking how new our country is. At the time I was born there were only forty-five states in the Union.

FIVE

Toys

I have found that a successful way to reach a long way back into one's memory is to write about toys. Nearly all of us had a favorite toy, or a toy that we didn't like for some reason, or even a toy that somehow influenced our lives. If you were very poor and had no toys, that, too, is part of your story. Maybe you lived in an isolated region where you didn't know what you were missing by not having any toys, or maybe your mother or father constructed a toy for you out of a piece of wood or a corncob.

As I mentioned in the foreword to this book, my mother, late in her life, wrote about a covered wagon trip which she made when she was five years old from Battle Lake, Minnesota to Independence, Missouri. At the end of that account she wrote the following story about a doll she received her first Christmas in Independence:

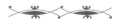

On Christmas Eve we had a nice entertainment at the church, and after that, the sheets were taken down from around a big

Christmas tree, which stood on one end of a platform. When it was uncovered, the children gasped at its beauty. There were strings of popcorn and bright red cranberries, and when someone lighted the tallow candles, it showed up the Christmas presents which the parents had brought for the children.

A big doll hung at the top of the tree, and that attracted my attention. She had a beautiful dress and was the main thing I could see. She was almost the last thing to be taken down and when they handed her to me, I almost collapsed. She had a beautiful wax head. Each child got a little sack of popcorn, besides their gifts. When the tree was unloaded, we were all anxious to go home to bed so that Santa Claus could come. We knew that we would each find our stockings in the morning where we had hung them. Santa always found the stockings, and put an apple, an orange, some mixed nuts, and hard candies in each one.

No one had furnaces in their homes, but some people had base burners that burned hard coal. They had doors on three sides, with lots of isinglass in them and when the fire was lighted they were beautiful. They were built so that they would throw the heat to the floor. I didn't want to put my lovely doll in a cold bedroom, so I wrapped her in a nice little blanket and put her in a doll bed behind the stove where she would be nice and warm. I could hardly wait to get downstairs in the morning to get my doll. But, to my consternation, she wasn't pretty anymore. The heat had melted her wax face. Of course my Christmas was spoiled. But the next day my father went to town and got a new head. This time he got a china head and I was happy after mother sewed it onto the cloth body. I treasured that doll for years.

My mother wrote that story when she was eighty-five years old, so I read it for the first time when I was a grown woman. My mother and I, I am sorry to say, were never close. I was born when her other three daughters were grown, and I believe she resented having to start bringing up a second family. Also, she had many other family pressures which I didn't fully comprehend at the time. Whatever the reason, and although I know we both wished it could have been different, my mother and I would probably have done better living on separate planets than in the same family. However, when I read that story about her doll I saw my mother as a little girl, thrilled with her doll and then devastated to find its beautiful head melted.

I cried off and on all day when I read about that doll for the first time, and I have always shed at least a few tears every time I have read the story since. For the rest of her life my feelings toward my mother were warmer as a result of that story because I knew that that little girl was somewhere inside the person whom I had known only as my mother. I make this personal comment only to indicate how much a parent's story can mean to a child, perhaps in ways the parent never suspects.

The first time I conducted a personal history writing class I read the story about my mother's doll as an example of the sort of thing I wanted the students to write. The next week everyone brought in a story about a toy, but memory association had been at work and three students also brought stories about heating devices they had remembered as a result of reading about my mother's base heater.

I have a story from my own childhood about a doll. I am going to tell it here for two reasons. First, because my feelings toward that doll are a perfect example of how our attitudes at various times in our lives reflect the era in which we live. Tying the events of your life to the period in which the events occurred can be a very important part of your story—a contribution to the history of the period as well as to the history of your family. Another reason for including the story is that, as I mentioned in ground rule number five, it is often good to tie events from your recent past or your present to events of your distant past. This story is a good example of that:

Do you remember "pickaninny" dolls? I believe I must have been four or five years old at the time that I received one from my cousin for Christmas. They were little black baby dolls with pigtails sticking out all over their heads. They didn't look like the real Negro babies I saw in their mothers' arms in stores and other public places. They were stereotypes of white people's fantasies of a Negro child. They looked rather like a baby Topsy.

Now I must make it clear that I do not remember at any time hearing Negroes spoken of with disrespect in my home. Although I grew up in the border state of Missouri, I don't remember hearing them called niggers, shiftless, lazy, or any of the other derogatory terms which have often been used to describe black people. I can honestly say that I don't believe I learned any prejudice against Negroes at home. Also, I don't remember knowing any Negroes personally. However, my attitude toward that little black doll reveals an enormous amount of prejudice and even blatant hostility surprising in one so young. Society must somehow have taught me in dozens of subtle ways that Negroes were not as good as white people.

When I opened the box containing the doll a profound sense of humiliation and rage that I can remember to this day swept over me. I slapped the doll and began to cry. My parents immediately asked what was wrong. "I thought Dorothy Dee liked me," I sobbed, "but she doesn't. She hates me!"

My mother took the lid off the box and lifted the doll out. Both she and my father tried to reassure me that Dorothy Dee did like me and that she and her mother had selected the doll for me because they thought it was cute. But I wasn't convinced. I grabbed the doll, ran up the stairs to the landing, which overlooked the living room, and threw the little black body down onto the living room floor as hard as I could and broke its head.

I hadn't thought about that doll for years—not until one of my classes was working on the civil rights assignment. I frequently write about my own life along with the class and while I was writing my civil rights story I remembered about the doll. I had written a different story for my toy assignment, but I decided to include the doll story too because it tied in so perfectly with my civil rights story. This made it possible for me to describe how my attitude had changed over the years. Such examples of personal growth will enrich your story. We all experience growth in various facets of our lives, and then there are other areas in which we seem to make little progress. When I remembered about the doll, I made a note "black doll" on the toy page of my memory bank to remind me to write the story later when I had time. This is how memory association works. Once you begin to jot down ideas, and particularly after you begin to write, you will find that your subconscious mind will toss up all sorts of stories which you had completely forgotten. You will have many surprising and interesting excursions into the past. Now here is my civil rights story:

Like many Americans, perhaps the majority, I didn't think much about the civil rights movement until Martin Luther King was shot. I, as I'm sure was the case with many Americans, realized then for the first time that our treatment of the American Negro had been morally outrageous. This realization was the beginning of my overcoming the prejudice of which I had until then been unaware. I must confess that my emotional freedom from prejudice, also like that of many Americans, was slower in coming than my mental freedom.

My final release came one night in 1964. I had directed a play in a community theater in Kansas City, Missouri. Anders, a very well educated black man (he had a Ph.D. in speech and was a high-ranking official in the local school system) played a role in the play. I got very well acquainted with him during the rehearsals and really ceased to think about his being either black or white. I just saw him as a dependable and talented member of the cast. Through him I met his wife, Jean, an attractive woman who had a master's degree in English.

After the last performance of the play we had a cast party at the suburban home of Anne, a cast member. Everyone had arrived except Anders and Jean. We were beginning to wonder if they had gotten lost when the front door bell rang.

Anne went to the door, spoke quietly to someone and then stepped out onto the porch and closed the door behind her. When she came back into the house Anders and Jean were with her. A few minutes later I was in the kitchen with Anne and she told me what had happened on the porch.

"That was a policeman at the door," she said. "He had stopped Anders and Jean just because they were driving in this neighborhood! They told him they were invited to a party at this address, but he said they would have to prove it and followed them up to the door and asked me if it were true. When I said it was," Anne's eyes filled with tears and her face turned bright red, "he asked if I would be responsible for their behavior while they were in the neighborhood. I nearly died I was so embarrassed!

"I said, 'No, I won't. They are well-educated, cultured adults and they are responsible for their own behavior, and furthermore they are my guests and I would like for you to leave my house and not humiliate them any more!' He said, 'Just doing my duty, ma'am.' They just stood there until he left and didn't say a word. I didn't know what to say to them."

Nor did I. In fact, I didn't know whether to say anything at all or to let it pass. Finally, I went over to Anders and Jean and whispered, "I can't tell you how sorry I am about all of this."

They both laughed nervously and said, "Don't worry about it. We're used to it. That sort of thing happens to us all the time."

When I began putting my book together I combined the story about my black doll and the civil rights story. Between the two I wrote this bridge:

It was many years before I understood why I was so insulted at receiving that doll. Throughout my childhood, teens, and young womanhood I never gave a thought to our treatment of Negroes. They had their place and I had mine and that was that. If asked, I would have sworn that I had no prejudice.

Go back and read the doll story, then the bridge, then the civil rights story and see how it all fits together. There will be more about combining and relating stories in the assignments in Chapter 29 "Revising and Pulling It All Together."

Some Dos and Don'ts

Several years ago I attended a time management seminar. At the beginning of the first session the instructor said, "Now you have paid a lot of money to attend this seminar. I wish I could say that it will be money well spent for all of you but, unfortunately, I can't. The follow-up that we have done on our seminars in various cities tells us that only a third of you will have the discipline to put into practice what you have learned here. The rest of you will just be out the $400 you have paid us." We all laughed and glanced nervously at one another, each confident of being part of the successful one-third.

I don't know for sure, of course, but I have a feeling that a follow-up on the readers of "how-to" books might yield similar statistics. I'm sure many people profit immeasurably from reading books that tell them how to do things, but I suspect that many other people are entertained and momentarily inspired but don't follow through on the advice the books offer. I admit that I have been guilty of this myself.

I hope there won't be a big "drop-out" ratio among the readers of this book. I hope every reader of the book will become a user of the book. I want many thousands of Americans to have the joy of giving their families the priceless gift of knowing something about their heritage.

By now you have read far enough to know how this book works. You know about memory association, about setting up your memory bank, about writing your story in small, manageable segments. You know that you don't have to worry about style, grammar, or continuity as you write. You know that this book is going to tell you how to revise your work and how to put it all together. You know the ten ground rules for writing your story. In short, you know enough to begin work on your story right now. You don't have to wait until you finish reading this book. I urge you to start immediately.

If you haven't already bought your notebooks and set up your memory bank and your writing book, please do so today, tomorrow at the latest. Making up the pages of your memory bank requires absolutely no skill and no inspiration. You can even do it while you're watching television.

Try to set aside at least half an hour each day to write. An hour is better, but half an hour will do very well. This is writing time—not revising time, not looking-up-words-in-the-dictionary time, not research or fact-finding time. All of that can be done later. Get something down on paper every day until you have finished all of the assignments in this book and any special chapters which you may want to write. I have found that if you will do this you can complete a book in thirty to forty weeks. The chapters on revision and research are purposely placed at the back of the book. That is where they belong. Writing comes first!

Another thing: Follow the instructions in this book. That may sound like a conceited thing for a book's author to say but I have seen writers create time-consuming and discouraging problems for themselves when they haven't followed instructions.

In nearly every one of my classes someone comes in with the first lesson written on every line of his or her notebook paper instead of on every other line. It's a natural mistake. We are accustomed to writing on every line when we write on lined paper, but it makes revision very difficult.

Another problem which arises is that someone occasionally tries to write practically the whole book at once, which makes a great deal of revision necessary. In my last class a woman brought in her first assignment, which was written about her birth. She started by writing a wonderful description of a little Missouri Ozark town. Then she wrote about the fact that her grandparents had been born in West Virginia, what her grandfather's occupation was, the fact that they moved to Kentucky, and so on. Next she wrote about her parents having been born in Kentucky, when and how they met, when they were married, and so on. Then she wrote that she was born in the little Ozark town. Meanwhile those of us who were listening to her read her story were trying to figure out what her grandparents' lives in West Virginia and her parents' lives in Kentucky had to do with the the little Ozark town. We kept thinking that perhaps she was going to say she had been born there, but we weren't sure. I hasten to add that everything she wrote was very interesting, but only part of our attention was on what she had written because our minds were busy wondering how it all fit together.

When I began trying to help her revise her work I discovered that her writing was single spaced so we couldn't add anything between the lines. Then I thought we might cut it apart and move the birth part near the beginning, with the description of the Ozark town, but unfortunately she had written on both sides of the paper so cutting wouldn't work. There was nothing for her to do but waste a lot of time copying much of what she had already written. How much better it would have been if she had written about her birth in one section, described the town in another section, and written about her parents and grandparents in still other sections and filed them temporarily in back of the appropriate memory bank pages. Then, with no trouble at all, she could have put them together in whatever order was clearest and most interesting.

Our descendants are going to love these books we are writing, but we must make sure that they are clear and well organized. Time is so precious in our complex civilization that nobody is going to spend a lot of time trying to figure out what we are talking about.

I have mentioned research once or twice, but I really haven't talked much about it. You probably won't have to do a great deal of research since you will be writing about things with which you are familiar. However, there will be times when you won't be quite sure about a fact or a date. There will be other times when you will want to write a little background information about an event so that your readers, who probably won't have personal knowledge of the event, can understand your part in it.

The chapter on research in the back of this book will tell you how you can quickly and easily find background material you need. Don't let the word "research" scare you. I'm not talking about plowing through mountains of material. A few hours, which will be easy and pleasant, will probably be all you will need to fill in necessary facts for your story.

When you are writing and have a fact or a date you want to check, leave a blank space on the page and make a red check to remind you that you want to look up something later. You can also use your memory page to jot down questions you want answered. This, too, should be done in red pencil so you won't overlook it when you are ready to do your research.

Of course, you may find that you enjoy your research so much that you will want to make it more extensive; that will be up to you. However, let me warn you—it's easy to get bogged down in research, not because it is so hard but because it can become so absorbing. That is why I am suggesting that you leave all of your research until after you finish your writing. That may sound odd, but it works very well. For example, in the assignment on "Where Were You on Momentous Days in History?" one man wrote about being in the Normandy landing on D day. He wrote about just his part in the invasion first, but then he wanted to add two or three paragraphs about the scope of D day, its place in history, and so on. A couple of hours in the library told him all he needed to know. I'll tell you exactly how he did it in the research chapter.

To recap:

1. **Set up your memory bank immediately.** Have it handy so you can jot down ideas which occur to you as you read this book.

2. **Write at least half an hour every day,** preferably at the same time each day.

3. **Make extra memory bank pages if you have special stories** to tell that are not covered by the assignments in this book.

4. **Start reading autobiographies as soon as you finish reading this book,** but don't let reading interfere with your writing. (Perhaps you can set up a system of rewards for yourself in which you give yourself the pleasure of reading an autobiography for an hour or so as soon as you finish your day's quota of writing.) Always have your memory bank handy so you can make notes of the memories which are sure to come to you as you read.

5. **Leave all of your research, revising, and assembling until after you have finished your writing.** You will find that all of the pieces will fit together like a beautiful mosaic.

SEVEN

Parents and Grandparents

Occasionally, students come to my classes with wonderful genealogical information about their families. I always envy them and so do members of the class, but the fact is that Americans who have extensive information about their ancestors are very much in the minority. Most of them, like me, know very little about their forebears. Many even know very little about the early lives of their own parents.

I don't think this indicates a lack of love among American family members. My own family is very close and loving. Recently, when one family member had a problem our combined long distance telephone bills for one month totaled nearly five hundred dollars as we all called frantically between various cities to see if we could help. No, I'm sure it isn't lack of love. I think it is just the "American way," part of the here-and-now syndrome that almost from the beginning has characterized our always-on-the move, upwardly mobile American society. Losing contact with our heritage is one part of the American way that I hope this book will help change—and that you can help change in your family by writing your own life story.

Of course, your parents (and perhaps your grandparents) will appear in many of the stories you write about your life, but you should, if possible, include some information about their character and background in a section of your book devoted entirely to them. In these hectic times when our society is changing so rapidly, our children, grandchildren, and future descendants can benefit from having the kind of solid link with the past that you can give them by writing about your life and what you can remember about your parents and their parents. Also, some background information on your parents will give your readers a better understanding of you and your life.

Make up a memory bank page for each parent and if possible for each grandparent. Put down names, dates and places of births, marriages, deaths, and more. Ask your parents or older members of your family, or for that matter even your contemporaries for information. They may, either by their own efforts or by accident, have collected information that you don't have and that they haven't thought to tell you about. If your parents and grandparents are dead, perhaps some of their friends are still living. If so, they would no doubt be delighted to answer your questions. Ask anyone you can think of who might have information. (Refer to the research chapter for tips on gathering information about your parents and grandparents.)

I have a perfect example of a surprising way that asking questions paid off for me. When I started my own story, I asked my sister some questions about our grandparents and great grandparents. She didn't know the answers, but after thinking a moment she said, "I think I may have some things that you might like to see. I haven't thought about them for years and I don't even remember what they are, but maybe they will help."

She went into the next room and came back with a file folder that contained a ten-page biography of our maternal grandfather and great grandfather! It had been written twenty years before by two second cousins whom we barely knew and who lived in a different state. They had been thoughtful enough to send my sister a copy. It had arrived at a time when she was busy with her own family and before she had developed an interest in family history. She appreciated our cousins' thoughtfulness but the biography had meant little to her at the time and she had simply put it in a file and forgotten about it. If I hadn't happened to ask her some specific questions she might never have thought to give me that biography. It might have stayed in her file until she died, at which time someone might have salvaged it or it might have been thrown away. The moral of this story is, *ask, ask, ask!*

Older members of your family may not offer information if you don't ask for it. They may think younger members of the family would not be interested or they may just not think to offer it because, like most people, they are busy with the present and take the past for granted.

Asking my mother questions yielded a very exciting story about the ancestor for whom I was named—Lois Cutler Sherman. I had always heard that I was named for Lois Cutler, but I had only the haziest idea of who she was. Thirty years ago, when my niece was born, my sister and brother-in-law named her Lois Elaine. The Lois was for me, not for Lois Cutler, but it got me to wondering about the name and I asked Mother to tell me something about Lois Cutler. "Well," said Mother, "I know she had a lot of interesting experiences with the Indians in Minnesota."

I urged Mother to write some of these experiences down, which she did. One of them is included in this chapter. I love the story and I hope you will too, but I am including it here primarily because I want to make a point about what not to do when you are writing your own story or that of your parents or grandparents. After you read the story I am going to point out a serious flaw in it. It is a flaw which could easily have been corrected and that I hope you will avoid in writing your story. This is the story my mother wrote:

Lois Cutler Sherman and her husband, Almon Sherman, homesteaded near Battle Lake, Minnesota. By the time they moved there many of the Indians were in a rather pitiful condition. They were hemmed in by white settlers and were unable to practice many of their old ways but hadn't partaken of white men's ways. They were just sort of in limbo. Lois had heard that the Indians in the small Sioux village near the homestead often didn't have enough to eat and were undernourished and sick. She felt sorry for them and wished she could help.

She finally gathered enough courage to pay a visit to the village to see if she could do anything for the Indians, particularly the children. She found that they were indeed in sad shape. For more than a year she made frequent visits to the village, taking food and helping the Indians when they were sick. The Indians showed their appreciation by giving her little gifts of things they had made.

One day Almon had gone to town and Lois and her two small children were alone on the farm. Lois happened to look out the window and saw ten or twelve Indian men whom she recognized as being from the village riding pell-mell toward the house. They jumped off their ponies and ran inside. Without saying a word, one unceremoniously grabbed Lois, another grabbed a child under each arm and the others gathered up as much furniture as they could carry.

They threw Lois and the children face down over their ponies, piled the furniture on the ponies, jumped on themselves, and raced toward a large grove of trees a few yards from the house. When they got well into the grove they stashed Lois and the children high in one tree and put the furniture in the tops of other trees. Then, again without saying a word, they jumped on their ponies and galloped away in the direction of their village.

Within minutes Lois and the children heard wild whoops and saw a great wave of Indians riding toward them. They were all wearing war paint, letting out terrifying yells, and carrying weapons and lighted torches. Most of the Indians rode past the house but four of them jumped off their ponies and stormed inside. They came back out in two or three minutes looking disgusted. Two of them set a torch to the house and all four of them jumped on their ponies and followed the rest of the Indians.

Lois and the children saw their home burn to the ground but at least they weren't in it and much of their furniture had been saved. Later, they found that the Indians had burned many homesteads and killed lots of white settlers that day.

Do you know what the flaw in this story is? If you don't, read it again and see if you can find it. Now turn back to the chapter of this book called, "Working on Your Assignments." In the ninth paragraph I mentioned the journalism rule that all stories must answer the questions who? what? why? how? where? and when? Let's see which of these questions the story answered.

What? A raid on white settlers by the Sioux Indians.

Why? Probably because of the Indians' desperation at having their way of life destroyed and their land taken over by the white settlers.

How? By burning homes and killing white settlers.

Where? Near Battle Lake, Minnesota.

But what about the all important **who?** and **when?** This story, like my grandfathers' biography, had been tucked away in a file (my file this time) for many years and taken out only when I started writing my life story. It tells a wonderful story about the woman for whom I am named but it doesn't give the slightest hint of my relationship to her. Was she my great grandmother? My great great grandmother? Who? The children were not mentioned by name. Was one my grandmother or perhaps my great grandmother? No doubt at the time Mother wrote the story she told me exactly who Lois Cutler was. However, that was thirty years ago and my life has been full and busy since then with little, if any, thought given to Lois Cutler. What Mother told me I simply don't remember.

My sisters and I tried to figure it out. We finally gathered enough genealogical data to discover that Lois Cutler was our great grandmother. She had only two children, so one of the children who was saved by the Indians in the story was none other than our own grandmother!

No wonder Mother was able to write the story in such vivid detail. It had undoubtedly been told to her by her mother, who lived through it. When we established that one of the little girls was my grandmother, one of my older sisters, all three of whom remembered our grandmother well, moaned, "Oh, think of the stories she could have told us if only we had thought to ask."

As to the "when" of the story—since an Indian "grabbed a child under each arm," the children must have been fairly small, the oldest, my grandmother, probably about six or seven years old. She was born in 1852 so that would have placed the story at approximately 1857 to 1859. I am currently researching Sioux history in the hope of pinning down the exact time of the raid, and discovering whether it was perpetrated by the Sioux nation or only by a relatively small band of Indians acting on their own.

I'm sure Mother had all of this information and she probably gave me all, or most, of it verbally at the time she wrote the story, but she didn't put it down on paper and neither did I. Remember, after you write each of your stories ask yourself, "Have I answered the questions who? what? why? how? where? and when?"

The following story, which one of my students wrote about her grandmother, reminds us of how rapidly time passes and how important it is for us to make an effort to preserve stories about the time when life in our country was so different from the way it is today (also to write about today because everything will be so different tomorrow).

This is a story of a beloved tax collector—no, that isn't a misprint; the word really is "beloved." (But this contrasts so drastically with the huge, faceless bureaucracy that collects our taxes today that it seems the tax collector in the story must have lived many generations ago). Yet her granddaughter, Jan, was only in her early thirties when she wrote this story in 1981. In fact, you probably read in your newspaper about an incident in which Jan was involved only a few years ago on a tragic night which is still vivid in the memory of Kansas citizens. She was one of many volunteer Red Cross workers who helped rescue people trapped in Kansas City's Hyatt Regency Hotel when its skywalks collapsed, killing dozens of people, and injuring many more. Jan wrote many stories about her grandmother, who must have been everything a grandmother should be—someone who was fun to visit, who cooked wonderful food for her grandchildren, and was always ready to listen to anything they wanted to talk about. Ruth Louella Eastman was only sixteen in 1918 when she married Wilbert Mason, a young Pennsylvania coal miner. Wilbert was killed in a mining accident, leaving his wife a widow at the age of twenty-five with three children, ranging in age from seven to less than a year. Here is one of Jan's "grandmother" stories:

One thing grandma did to help cope with her difficult situation after grandpa died was to run for the job of tax collector in Lincoln Township of Somerset County, Pennsylvania. She won the election and was re-elected every time there was an election until she chose to retire more than thirty-five years later.

She had her office in her home, except for the days when she would "sit" at the schools or stores or some other public building in the little towns in her township. Also, she sometimes went "on the road," visiting in the homes and trying to collect delinquent taxes. Many of the coal miners who had bought their homes from the coal company and then lost their jobs and gone on public assistance became delinquent in their taxes. Grandma always felt guilty about having to collect taxes from such unfortunate persons.

Being a widow was not the only serious challenge that Grandma had to face. Shortly after her husband's death, she began to experience severe pain and paralysis in her back and neck from her waist up. It was discovered that she had a rare, and at that time, untreatable form of arthritis. Eventually, the cartilage between the vertebrae fused and Grandma became stooped and could not straighten up. I never knew her except when she had a distinct curvature of her spine and could not twist her neck or body. She had to lean her whole body back if she wanted to look you in the eye and to turn her whole body if she wanted to look in another direction.

She never complained about her arthritis and paralysis except one day she said she would be glad when she got to Heaven and could straighten up and breathe deeply. And once in awhile she would be self-conscious about her curvature when she was trying on clothes in a department store. I also recall that toward the end of her life she had a preoccupation with whether or not they would have to break her back to lay her out flat in her coffin.

Jan went on to say that her grandmother was finally laid in her coffin when she was sixty-nine years old. Hundreds of people, many of whom she had always referred to as "my taxpayers," came to pay their respects to the valiant, misshapen little tax collector.

Most of the members of the class were wiping their eyes when Jan read the following closing lines of this story about her grandmother:

I miss her very much but much of her still lives on in my mind and heart. I'm so proud to have had such a wonderful grandma. She always seemed young to me!

Probe your memory for facts about your parents and grandparents. Can you remember them when you were three or four years old? Was your mother a good cook? Did she like cooking, keeping house? Was she pretty? What was your father's job? Did he like it? Was he handsome? What was their relationship to each other? How did they discipline you? Did they play with you? You won't remember everything at once, of course, but one memory will trigger another. For example, even as I type this I remember something I hadn't thought of for years. On Sunday morning, before church, I used to stand on the rockers on the back of my father's rocking chair and look over his shoulder while he read the funnies to me. Memory association will work like this for you too. Many things will come to you as you write. I'm sure that having read this far in this book, you have already remembered many long forgotten incidents. Jot reminders of all these memories on the appropriate memory bank page—don't let them get away.

The next story is a wonderful demonstration of ground rule number eight—share a little wisdom with your descendants. Part of that rule is "but don't preach!" The writer of this story didn't preach but she did a wonderful job of demonstrating two completely different kinds of behavior, either one of which could be a mirror in which a reader might see himself or herself. And how could a reader resist looking on the bright side of things after reading about the mother in this story?

I don't know whether to describe Mother as happy or joyful— perhaps cheerful would be best. She always looked on the positive side of life. If she had half a glass, she not only saw the glass as half full but she expected that more could and would come to fill it. Dad, on the other hand, saw the glass as half empty. In fact, he would have pronounced whatever was in it "nearly gone."

Every night at 5:14, Dad would come in the French doors from the garage announcing himself, as usual, by asking, "Is dinner ready?"

"Not yet," Mother would answer from the kitchen.

Then Dad went to hang up his hat, stopping at the kitchen door to remind Mother, "You know I haven't eaten anything since breakfast, so I'm hungry when I get home." This was said in a martyred tone, although he was the one who decided that if he ate lunch, he wasn't hungry for dinner. He not only skipped lunch, he thought everyone should. (I remember some horrible vacation trips when it might be two o'clock before he stopped for lunch, after scolding his hungry horde for their alleged gluttony.)

One evening when I was about eleven Mother assured Dad, as always, "I know, John. Dinner will be ready by six." That was an inviolate law at our house, or a cranky Dad got downright cantankerous. Dad settled in his chair by his radio to read the newspaper until 5:59. At six he would be at the table.

I was Mother's kitchen aide. I had set the dining table and was returning from putting on the salads when Mother said, "Just look at the color coming into the kitchen." She stepped into the adjoining laundry room to look out its west window. "Oh, there's a magnificent sunset!" she exclaimed. She dashed back to the kitchen to check the stove and oven. "Come on," she said, "we'll drive up to the hills to see the sunset."

I was thunderstruck. You didn't stop dinner preparations to go see a sunset—especially at our house. "But what about dinner?" I asked, standing there like a stone. "It will take care of itself," Mom answered. "Hurry!"

Outside, the sky was bathed in a red glow, but I was too nervous to appreciate it. Dad would have a fit if he heard Mom backing the car out. We scooted up Claremont Avenue to where the great white wedding cake of the Claremont Hotel perched at the base of the Berkeley hills. "I think this street will take us up to the hills above the sunset," said Mom, as she chose her road. At first there were houses, then the road swerved down into the glen, but finally it turned and took us up a steep grade toward a hilltop. The world around us was turning crimson. When Mother stopped the car at the top of the hill, we got out to see a world on fire.

As the sun descended toward the Golden Gate, it had found an opening in the low overhanging clouds. The sun's rays lit up those clouds from underneath, turning them to a fiery red. That brilliance, in turn, was reflected on San Francisco Bay below— and in everything else. We were in a bowl of blazing light.

Slowly the fires began to burn out, leaving only gray ash overhead, while still firing up the bay and the buildings of San Francisco. When only a few embers remained, we silently got in the car and sped home in a still-rosy glow. Dad would be angry but some things were worth taking a risk.

Perhaps time waited while the sun-fire burned itself out because to my surprise mother and I were putting dinner on the table just as Dad sat down at six. He didn't know the world had been on fire, and that Mother had taken me to see it burn.*

Writing about your parents may bring back sweet memories or bitter memories, or a mixture of the two, depending on your relationship to them. Whatever your memories, strive for complete honesty. Perhaps you understand your parents now better than you once did. Perhaps you now know things that you never suspected at the time; perhaps you realize now that your parents often deprived themselves in order to give you things they wanted you to have. Perhaps, if your memories are bitter ones, you now understand why your parents behaved as they did. Put down the facts as honestly as you possibly can. Your adult perspective will enhance your story. Remember, your parents and grandparents were individuals as well as parents and grandparents. Try to present them as individuals.

One of my students wrote that she liked to help her mother in the kitchen "as much as she would let me." That little phrase suggested there was more to the story. What did it mean? Did her mother refuse to let her help because the young girl always made a mess? Did she refuse her help because she, herself, was a perfectionist and thought that she was the only one who could cook it properly? Did she love to cook and want to be the queen of the kitchen without being bothered by her children? I, along with other students in the class, asked all of these questions, and we pointed out that just one additional sentence explaining that statement could be very helpful in describing her mother's character.

Are you like your parents in various ways? Are you like them in ways that you like or in ways that you dislike? Mentioning these similarities might give added dimension to your story. In the forward to this book I mentioned that I adored my father but was never close to my mother. Yet now that I am grown and old hurts are somewhat dulled I have to admit that, for the most part, the characteristics which have served me best during my life are those which I believe I inherited from my mother. I did, however, inherit one very valuable characteristic from my father, a need to travel and to see and do unusual things.

The following story is an example of how an adult perspective made me realize that I had inherited a spirit of adventure from my father:

I remember hearing my father say that as a boy he was constantly reading "dime novels," cheap pulp fiction of the day which glorified the American West. His parents considered the books trash and Daddy had to read them secretly. Like thousands of other boys in the last half of the nineteenth century his great dream was to see and explore the West. In 1897, after he graduated from high school in Kalamazoo, Michigan, he left home against his parents' wishes and embarked on a western adventure.

As I was growing up I heard him tell about living the life of a wanderer for two years and it used to embarrass me terribly because I didn't want people to think my father had been a tramp.

It wasn't until one day in August, 1950, when I was sitting on the deck of a ship bound for Germany that I realized that I was doing exactly what my father had done. I had left home against my parents' wishes to go off seeking adventure. I was going to Germany for two years to work as a civilian employee of the U.S. Army. It was during the occupation of Germany when the country was still devastated and block after block of its major cities were nothing but rubble.

My parents were determined that I shouldn't go. They had good reason to be concerned. It was at the height of the Cold War when we thought there was a very real possibility that the Russians might attack West Germany, but I had to go. Although I was very young during World War II, I was completely engrossed in the war and fascinated by what could have prompted the barbarism of the Germans. I had to go to Germany and see for myself what had happened to the country and to try to understand the German people.

As I sat on the ship that day I was thinking about the great adventure on which I was embarking. What would happen to me in Germany? What would I find there? I thought, "Why, this is exactly what Daddy did. He ran away to explore the West just as I am running away to explore Germany."

The only difference between us was that I was doing my adventuring in a more lady-like way. He stole rides on freight trains, worked on ranches, and slept in haystacks. I, on the other hand, got myself a job with a decent salary, and a lot of built-in protections before going out to do my exploring. "Other than that," I thought, "we're just alike."

I began trying to remember the few stories I had heard Daddy tell about the West. I could recall only three brief incidents. One was about the night he was hitching a ride on top of a boxcar and fell asleep and rolled off the train in Limon, Colorado and cracked his skull. Another was the time he hid in a boxcar while the train was stopped. It was only half filled with railroad ties so Daddy thought this would give him plenty of room to move around during the trip.

He moved around all right, but not the way he had expected. Whoever loaded the ties had forgotten to secure them and when the train started going up and down the hills and mountains of Colorado the ties constantly shifted and Daddy had to scramble desperately to stay out of their way and keep from being rammed. I remember hearing him say, "I was never still for more than a minute or two at a time." The harrowing trip lasted three hours. It could have been a scene out of a Robert Redford movie!

The only other Western story I could remember was that Daddy signed on for a month to work on a large wheat ranch about sixty miles from Denver. He was to get room and board and wages. In those days, to get to Denver, the nearest town to the ranch, required several hours on horseback or in a horse-drawn vehicle. There was no running down to McDonald's and picking up a hamburger if the ranch food was insufficient, which it was. It was, in fact, ridiculously sparse, particularly for men who were working hard from before daylight until after dark.

Every morning at breakfast the rancher's wife fried the eggs very hard so they could be cut in two, and each man was served half an egg. For several days the men ate in silence. Finally, at the beginning of the second week one of the men rebelled. "Damn it," he exploded. "I want something to eat!" He jumped up from the table, ran around to the other side, grabbed the rancher by the front of his shirt and shouted, "I'm sick of this, you tight son-of-a-bitch! You tell your wife to give me a whole egg."

The rancher, without taking his eyes off the man, said calmly to his wife: "Aw, give the hog a hull egg and let him eat 'til he busts."

I began to dream about the adventure stories my father and I could exchange when I got home. I was sure I would have marvelous stories to tell, and I now realized that he did too. But my father died suddenly while I was in Germany so we two adventurers never had a chance to swap tales. My father's stories of the Old West died with him.

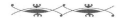

ASK, ASK, ASK!
WRITE, WRITE, WRITE! When you write about parents and grandparents make sure that whenever possible you write about them in relationship to you, in relationship to each other, and in relationship to their own times.

EIGHT

It Wasn't Always Easy for Our Ancestors to Write Their Stories

For eight years I devoted approximately half of my time to editing the *Overland Journal*, which is a quarterly magazine published by the Oregon–California Trails Association. It was a fascinating job. Before I started, all I knew about the Oregon and California trails was what I had seen in the movies, and working on the magazine helped me discover that much of that was wrong. The true stories, which are to be found in the diaries, reminiscences, and letters written by the immigrants who went over the trails, are far more interesting than anything ever devised for the movies. We know of more than two thousand existing diaries, and more are turning up all the time.

Now this is where I'm going to, as the kids say, "lay a guilt trip" on you if you happen to be thinking that writing your stories will be too much trouble. In one of the trail diaries a woman wrote the following:

I didn't write in my diary yesterday. I hate to miss a day, but I just couldn't do it yesterday. It was dark by the time we found a place to camp and both George [her husband] and I were too tired to build a fire to melt the ink.

Another woman wrote:

The color of the ink in my journal will be changing all of the time from now on. I thought I brought enough ink for the entire journey, but have completely run out. From now on I'm going to pick berries and squeeze the juice out of them and use it for ink. The color of my writing will depend on the kind of berries I'm able to find.

Now there's a lady who really wanted to write the story of her life!

Many trail letters and journals have been found that make it obvious that the writer had run out of paper and was unable to get more. Writers sometimes wrote horizontally across the page in the usual manner and then wrote vertically over the same page. This makes the writing hard to read, but with patience one can make it out. Knowing the effort the writer made to record every scrap of information possible, one can't dream of refusing to take the trouble to decipher the writing no matter how long it takes.

Many people went to a great deal of trouble to tell us about our country's past. Can we do any less for our descendants when we have all of the pencils, ball-point pens, and paper we need—perhaps even a typewriter or a computer?

NINE

The Accomplishment of Which You Are the Most Proud

I have always enjoyed teaching this assignment because it motivates students to dig deep inside and come face to face with what is best in themselves. Few of us do anything really spectacular during our lifetime, such as developing an important invention, making an outstanding scientific discovery, producing a major work of art, or founding a great institution. However, all of us do things in the normal course of our daily lives which require courage, special effort, conquest of self, ingenuity, perseverance, sacrifice, or use of special skills. Often we take these qualities for granted and don't give ourselves enough credit for some of our accomplishments. Now is the time for a little stocktaking, for giving yourself a pat or two on the back.

Chances are you will find that you will recall several candidates for the accomplishment of which you are the most proud. Jot them all down as you remember them. I have placed this chapter in the first half of the book because as you sift through your memories, trying to decide which are your most significant achievements, you are sure to remember many incidents which will furnish the basis for several segments of your story.

One word of warning. You may find that the achievement you consider to be your most significant is not the same as the one others consider the most significant. The story later in this chapter by the woman who started the prayer chain is an excellent example of this fact. She received a lot of praise from many people for that effort, but you will notice that she, herself, does not consider it her most significant achievement. In his beautiful short story, *The Crock of Gold*, James Stephens wrote, "The head does not hear anything until the heart has listened." Listen with your heart as you select the accomplishment of which you are the most proud. All that matters is what you think and feel based on your own values. What others think doesn't count.

Perhaps you will want a chapter describing in detail several of the achievements of which you are the most proud. More likely, though, you will find that each special achievement will become a major part of some other chapter of your book. But write the story of each of your favorite achievements and file them in back of your memory bank page marked "The Accomplishment of Which I Am Most Proud." Later you can incorporate these stories into your book wherever they fit.

Here are some examples of significant achievements about which students have written. You will notice that none of them is the sort of thing that is likely to receive extensive press coverage, but all are beautiful achievements. They will all make fascinating and inspiring reading for the children, grandchildren, and great grandchildren of the writers. Perhaps they will remind you of some accomplishments about which you will want to write.

A Jewish woman wrote about her daughter, Edith, who was in love with a young Gentile. Here is a brief excerpt from her story:

We could not help liking Russel. He was pleasant to us and considerate of Edith, but we had been taught since childhood that it was wrong for Jews to marry outside the Jewish faith. When persons are united by a common culture, religious belief or tradition, they are likely to harbor hostile feelings toward an individual who is "different."

She went on to write that when her daughter announced her intention to marry Russel, her husband, Herb, ordered the young man out of their house and forbade Edith to see him again. Then she described in detail a miserable year in which she and her husband knew that Edith was seeing Russel regardless of their wishes. The parents were distraught at the thought that Edith might marry without their blessing and that they might lose her forever. Yet their prejudice against the young man persisted in spite of the fact that he, having no religion of his own, was quite willing for his children to be reared as Jews. Her story continues:

One day as I was worrying about Edith and Russel I began thinking about all of the things that separate and cause tension between the people of the world. Suddenly, I realized that I could no longer contribute to a terrible division in my own family.

That night I told Herb how I felt. I said, "Those two are in love and they shouldn't have to feel guilty about it. We are the ones who are guilty. We do a lot of talking and listen to a lot of talk about brotherhood. It's the theme of organizations, synagogues, temples, and churches, but here we are facing this challenge in our own lives and we back away from brotherhood. I'm ready to offer the kids help and love instead of putting a barrier between us."

Herb was silent for a moment. I sensed his inner struggle. He is a good man and was not being obstinate. He was struggling with something he had been taught since childhood. "Couldn't we just take a first step," I asked, "even if we don't feel like it, and invite Russel to our home?" Finally, Herb agreed.

A week later Russel came to our house for dinner. He was so thrilled by our acceptance that his joy was contagious. It was the beginning of my husband and me being loosed from the bonds of prejudice.

Edith and Russel have been happily married for eleven years and we have three lovely grandchildren. It's frightening to think of the happiness of which we might have deprived them and of how our own hearts might have hardened if we had continued to turn our backs on them.

Some of our Jewish friends disagree with our acceptance of our son-in-law. I do not criticize them for their belief. I know how ingrained it is. I know that some Christian religions also forbid or discourage marriage outside their church. I cannot judge anyone else. I can only say that my husband and I did what was right for us.

I feel that the most significant accomplishment of my life was taking that first little step away from prejudice and urging my husband to join me in inviting Russel to dinner. It may not seem to be much to others, but it saved our family from terrible heartache and nothing is more important to me than that.

The woman who wrote this beautiful story put it behind the proudest accomplishment page in her memory bank where she left it until she was ready to put her book together. Then with just a few changes she incorporated it into a chapter about the marriages of her two children.

When her book was finished she said, "You know, I'm glad we had that assignment on our most important accomplishment. I really had never thought of what I did as being a great accomplishment, but after thinking about it, I realize that it was quite an accomplishment, and I'm kind of proud of it. If I hadn't given that assignment a lot of thought I probably would have just written, 'My daughter, Edith, and her husband, Russel, were married on June 8, 1970.'" (Remember ground rule number four—Don't let your story be just a sterile recital of events.)

She added, "I let Edith read it, and you can't imagine how touched she was. I had never told her as many of the details of Herb's and my struggle as I put in the story, and it meant an awful lot to her."

A little soul searching and soul sharing can add immeasurably to the value of your book just as it did to this woman's.

Another student, a man, wrote about a hobby which provided him with an accomplishment of which he was especially proud. He had been a ham radio operator for forty years. Instead of using his time, skill, and equipment to visit with other ham operators, he devoted all of his "on-the-air" time to helping people communicate with loved ones from whom they were separated. Scientists, technicians, Army, Navy, and State Department personnel, missionaries, and many others received his help.

Some were in such isolated places as Antarctica where ships or planes could not deliver mail for months at a time. Others were in remote weather stations north of Greenland. One young American woman who had married a rancher and lived in the Australian bush called her parents in California once a month. People in dozens of foreign countries have been helped and are still being helped by this man.

They reach him via radio which, of course, is free. Then he plugs the call into a telephone line on a collect call to their loved ones in the United States. The folks at home pay only for the long distance calls from his home in Missouri to their home. He often works late at night or early in the morning to run patches when the telephone rates are cheapest so he can save his customers money. He modestly stated that many people may not see this as a great achievement but that it has given him a great deal of pleasure to help literally thousands of people over four decades.

One woman's favorite accomplishment came after she had retired from thirty-five years of teaching school. She was instrumental in starting a meals-on-wheels program for the elderly in her rural area, the fourth such program in the country.

Another woman pointed to her work with Al-Anon teenagers, the children of alcoholics, as the accomplishment of which she is most proud.

A forty-five-year-old woman who was confined to a wheelchair as a result of an accident wrote that when she first discovered she would never walk again she was consumed with self-pity. To compound her problems, her husband was transferred to another city soon after her accident, and she had to move away from supportive friends and family. Alone and without friends in a new city she became so despondent that she considered suicide. Here are a few lines from her story:

My life became an agony of loneliness, depression, and self-pity. Although more than anything else I wanted to kill myself, I couldn't bring myself to do it. Finally, one day I realized that I couldn't go on another day as I was. I either had to live or die. I couldn't continue to just exist in misery. I analyzed the steps I would have to take in order to start living again, and in sorting out all of my emotions, I realized that the one which was most destructive was my self-pity.

She went on to tell what was involved in overcoming her self-pity and described how through her church she organized a prayer chain. She wrote movingly of the vital importance this chain played in her own life and in the lives of hundreds of other people in many states and several foreign countries. Here is the concluding sentence of her story:

But the greatest accomplishment of my life was not establishing the prayer chain. My greatest accomplishment was finding the courage to throw off my self-pity.

(Remember ground rule number eight?—Share a little wisdom with your descendants.)

A retired railroad brakeman wrote about the monumental task he and other railroad men performed in keeping the railroads, which were then the life-blood of the United States, running during World War II. Here are three paragraphs from his story:

It's almost impossible for today's automobile and airplane oriented kids to understand the role the railroads played in World War II. I don't suppose anybody will ever know the exact amount of freight or the number of people that we carried in those days. The mass of humanity on the move was almost unbelievable. Servicemen going home on leave or back to join their outfits, wives and sweethearts visiting the training camps, businessmen going to Washington and other cities to work on war contracts. Many times in the coaches there was standing room only, and I have seen hundreds of servicemen lying outside on the platforms trying to get a little sleep.

There was a terrible shortage of engines and cars. Every piece of rolling stock that could possibly hold together was put into service no matter how old it was. Decrepit, overworked equipment would break down and there was little material for repairs because there was a shortage of everything, but no amount of effort was too great for us if it meant keeping the trains running. We all knew that our job was one of the most important in the country. There was a wonderful camaraderie among the railroad men.

I'm proud that I was part of that great World War II railroad effort. I consider it the greatest single contribution of my life.

I myself had almost forgotten the role that railroads played in World War II, and I was there. If I needed reminding, how much more do the current generation and future generations need to have than this man's story written for them?

These are just a few samples of the accomplishments of which some of my students were the most proud. Does one of them spark a memory of your own accomplishments? I'm sure you have many to your credit. Think about them. Write about them. Enrich your story with them.

TEN

Create Your Own Assignments

As I said in my introduction to this book, the assignments list I have made can't possibly cover all of the stories in your life. I know you have stories to tell that I couldn't have dreamed of when I compiled the list. What are they? What experiences, opportunities, problems, or solutions to problems, even tragedies, can you write about that make your life completely different from anyone else's?

This is a hard question to answer because everyone's life is unique. No two lives are alike and yet all lives are somewhat similar. Although no two lives are exactly alike in their rich detail, many lives share similarities in time, place, human needs, social situations, problems, and joys peculiar to their sex, and more. It is fascinating to consider how much our lives are alike and yet how totally different they all are.

In the chapter called "Working on Your Assignments" I told how George Papashvily, an emigrant from Georgia, devoted an entire chapter of his book *Anything Can Happen* to his search in the United States for someone who could speak his native language. Needless to say, I could never have thought of an assignment page for such a situation. Yet, it was one of the most poignant and charming chapters of his book. It is very possible that you have something so special to tell about your life that I haven't thought of an assignment page for it and yet for you to omit it would be a very great loss to your readers.

One man, the only blind person who has ever attended one of my writing classes, knew immediately what he would write for this assignment. He was a retired physician and minister. In class he had written about his many experiences as a medical missionary to India. However, for his special assignment he wrote about something that happened to him after he retired. At the age of seventy he lost his sight quite suddenly. (He was seventy-nine when he was in my class.) He wrote about the shock, the adjustment to blindness, and his final victory over the blindness and its accompanying despair. He wrote, "In place of eyesight, I received insight, and in place of the emptiness I felt when I first discovered that I would be blind for the rest of my life, I received a portion of the Holy Spirit which has given me much greater spiritual joy than I ever experienced during all of my years as a minister."

Incidentally, this man was an inspiration to all of us. He had learned to type when he was seventy-two, two years after he lost his sight. We asked him how he had the courage to take on such a learning task so late in life. He answered, "Well, I had to, because when I couldn't see any longer my writing just scrawled all over the page and nobody could read it. I couldn't write to my children or to my friends."

Of course, we all knew he didn't have to learn to type at all. He could have given up on corresponding with friends and relatives and no one would have blamed him. He *chose* to learn to type and to stay in the mainstream of life in spite of his physical challenge. For this assignment an eighty-year-old woman who, with her family, had emigrated from Scotland when she was twelve years old wrote about the most difficult single adjustment the family had to make to their new country. She wrote:

The hardest adjustment my family had to make when we came to America wasn't anything one might expect. It wasn't the language; we all spoke English. It wasn't the problem of making a living in a new country. My uncle immigrated before we did and had arranged a job for my father before we came. It wasn't even making new friends and adapting to a new culture. The most difficult adjustment we had to make on our arrival in America was living in a house built of wood! In Scotland all of the houses and other buildings were built of stone. We had never seen frame and shingle houses before, and we were terrified of going to sleep at night for fear we'd all burn up if the wood caught fire.

It will sound strange to Americans, but the first few nights we were in our new home my mother and father and my brother and sister and I took turns sitting up at night so we could awaken the rest of the family if the house should catch fire.

Another "special page" was written by a man who was a German immigrant, and although millions of other Germans lived through the same experience and it was, therefore, not really unique, it is a story for which I had given no assignment. It is also a story which tells a bit of very interesting German history which future and even present generations can profit from reading. Here is his story:

I write this story for my assignment for my special page because it was a turning point in my life, the time that made me come to America. Partly, also I write it because I am thinking about this time often now while inflation is getting worse and worse in the United States. Sometimes I want to get on television and say to labor people, "please don't ask so much," and to business people, "please don't gouge so much," and to all American people, "please don't buy things you don't need and maybe prices will go down," and to the government, "please stop squandering our money." You see, I don't think Americans know yet what inflation can mean. Oh sure, we spend a little more here and a little more there but still most of us have enough money for what we need. But where will it end? Maybe not where it ended in Germany when I was a young man, but who knows? Anyway, I want to tell you about inflation in Germany in 1922.

I was a young man of twenty. I was working as a machinist's helper in a large factory in Munich, but it was almost no use to work because the money meant nothing. We no longer got our pay in pay envelopes because no envelope was big enough to hold all of the money that was for one week's work. I used to take a grocery bag from my landlady to collect my wages, but even with a whole grocery bag full of money I could not buy a pair of shoes.

Then it got so bad that instead of paying people every week they began to pay people every day so they could spend the money before it lost more value. In some factories—one very near where I worked—they started paying two times every day—noon and night. At noon the workers' wives came to the plant and received their husbands' wages for the morning from the paymaster. Then they went out and spent the money that afternoon because they knew it would buy more then than it would buy the next day. At the close of work the husbands would collect their money for the afternoon and give it to their wives to spend the next morning because it would not buy so much in the afternoon. The women used all of their time spending the money as fast as they could while the men were working all day for money that was worth almost nothing.

I had no family to keep me in Germany so I decided to leave. I quit my job and went to Bremerhaven hoping to get a boat to America, but even though I had a whole suitcase full of marks it wasn't enough to buy even a steerage class ticket. Also, I had no visa for America so I would have to pay someone to smuggle me ashore. I tried to get a job on a ship but lots of other people had the same idea and there were not enough jobs for all. Finally, I stowed away in a ship, and that is how I got to America.

I was what we call an illegal alien for twelve years, but I didn't feel illegal. I only felt very happy and built up a nice little restaurant business in an old streetcar. We served good German food and lots of other German immigrants liked to eat there. I got married and had two sons. I never felt that I was near getting caught by the immigration authorities, but I wanted to become an American citizen so I went back to Germany and in 1933 I came back to America legally.

Five years later I became a citizen, and I love this country. I have built two good businesses and now I am retired and my wife and I are happy doing just whatever we want to do, but what I want to do most now is to tell other Americans we must take care of our wonderful country. I don't know how to go about it though but at least I am writing this little story and maybe someone who reads it will know how to tell about the dangers of inflation to more people. The trouble is maybe the people in this class and my wife and our two sons and their families will be the only ones who read it. Anyway, who can understand such an inflation if they have not lived through it?

What are your unique stories? I'm sure you have some. Are they funny? Sad? Inspiring? Do they, like the story about Germany's inflation, illuminate some relatively unknown bit of history?

ELEVEN

Where Were You on Important Days in History

A woman in one of my classes told a charming story. Several years ago, when her granddaughter was only four years old, my student was telling her daughter how proud and grown up she felt the first time her mother let her help clean the chimneys of the family's kerosene lamps. Her little granddaughter overheard the conversation and asked, "Grandma, why didn't you just turn on the electric lights?"

Her grandmother answered, "Well, honey, we didn't have electric lights in those days."

The little girl then asked, "Why didn't you call the telephone company and have them come and fix your lights?"

My student laughed and answered, "Honey, we didn't have any telephones either."

The little girl stared thoughtfully at her grandmother for a moment and then asked, "Grandma, did you know Moses?"

I think that little girl spoke for most of us. We have very little concept of time outside our own life span. In my classes I am constantly amazed by the things my students remember. I had a particularly interesting experience in this regard a couple of years ago. I remember very well when I was quite young seeing the Jeannette MacDonald/Clark Gable movie, *San Francisco*, that depicted the San Francisco earthquake. I was enthralled by the film but I had no idea that the earthquake had occurred in the relatively recent past. It seemed to me that it had happened long, long ago. I was absolutely dumbfounded, but also thrilled, when a survivor of the earthquake turned up in one of my classes, and she was only seventy-seven years old!

She wrote the following memories of that momentous day for this assignment:

On Wednesday, April 18, 1906, I was asleep in my parents' San Francisco home when the earthquake hit. I was six years old and shared a double bed with my four-year-old sister. I awakened when I heard a terribly loud noise and felt my bed moving from one wall to the other. I heard my little sister scream and looked over and discovered that she was not in the bed beside me but rolling against the wall on the floor. I had no idea what was happening; I don't think I had ever heard of an earthquake.

Mixed in with the other noises, I heard my mother scream, "Get the children!" Everything seemed to be crashing down around us.

My little sister and I had a terrible time trying to get to my parents' room. The floors were tilted at about a thirty-five degree angle and we had to climb uphill in order to get out of our room. My parents met us in the living room where the heating stove had been tipped on its side and its chimney had fallen onto the floor, blowing soot all over the room. Broken glass from the windows and plaster from the ceilings and walls were everywhere. Somehow my mother and father managed to get my sister and me into coats and shoes and into the street.

Just as I remember loud crashing inside the house, as walls, furniture, chimneys, and windows tumbled around us, I remember complete quiet when we got outside. The quake had stopped and the after shocks, which were to follow, had not yet begun. People were everywhere but no one was saying anything. They seemed to be in a state of complete shock and speechless panic.

Every house on the block had been badly damaged. Several, like ours, were tilted at an angle. Some had no fronts. There was a large wardrobe lying on its back in the middle of the street.

Suddenly, a man's shout broke our stunned silence. "Get out of here," he yelled as he came running around the corner from a side street. "There's fire all around you."

We looked up and saw smoke and flames rising over the housetops in three directions. Many early risers had already lit their kerosene lamps and started fires in their stoves. Lamps had been broken and stoves had collapsed, spreading flames. Just then a heavy after-shock jarred people into activity. More parts of houses fell into the streets.

I heard the adults talking about where we should go. Since San Francisco is a peninsula and surrounded on three sides by water, there seemed to be only one direction to walk—south. So all of the neighbors started walking. We hurried as fast as we could but there were many children who couldn't go very fast and several adults were carrying babies. One man was carrying two little girls. We kept hoping to get to a safe place, but nobody really knew for sure where that would be. When you're running from a flood or a fire you have some idea of which direction to go, but you never know where an earthquake will strike next.

More people joined us as we walked, and all along our route there was terrible destruction. We saw many places where the streets had chasms six feet wide in them. One house had completely sunk into the ground. Only the tops of the second floor windows, or perhaps they were third floor windows, were visible above the ground.

It was nearly noon when we reached South San Francisco and we were exhausted and terribly hungry. Nobody had eaten since dinner the night before.

In a way, South San Francisco had been a good choice. It wasn't built up so much so there were very few buildings to fall on us if a quake should hit. In another way, it hadn't been a good choice. The army, which had a big post outside San Francisco, set up soup lines and brought blankets and other necessities to the people who had taken refuge in San Francisco's many parks, but they didn't think about people having gone to South San Francisco. Although the people in South San Francisco tried to help us as much as possible by giving us food and inviting us into their homes, there just weren't enough homes, nor was there enough food, to accommodate the hundreds of people who had fled there. It was the next day before the army heard about us and came to our rescue. I shall always remember the wonderful sight of a long line of mule-pulled army wagons suddenly appearing on the horizon. The wagons were loaded with food, cots, tents, and blankets.

Approximately 700 people lost their lives in the earthquake and 250,000 were left homeless. The quake destroyed 28,000 buildings and four square miles in the center of the city.

San Francisco, as nearly everyone knows, is situated on the San Andreas Fault, which seismologists say is one of the worst possible locations in the world for a city. Not many of us are left who remember the 1906 earthquake; soon we will all be gone. Young people, even though they have heard about the earthquake, can't comprehend the destruction and think it can never happen to them. Maybe it never will, but seismologists and geologists say another major quake is long overdue.

I have visited San Francisco many times since I moved to the midwest forty years ago, and when I go there I, like any other tourist, always go to the top of Telegraph Hill and look down on the wonderful city. But as I stand there, drinking in the view, I can't help thinking, "It's so beautiful, but so treacherous underneath."

The paragraph about the extent of damage caused by the earthquake was added at my suggestion. I had no idea myself how much damage the quake had caused and I felt sure my student's readers wouldn't either. It's a good idea not to assume too much knowledge about an event on the part of your readers. In order for them to understand your participation in it you have to tell them a little bit about it. Most of us remember where we were on important days in history and it is vital that we write our memories because history books talk only in grand sweeps. They don't tell the real story of historical events because the real story can be told only in the lives of the people who lived through them. When you write about an event, write about how you felt at the time, and remember you certainly don't have to have been a participant in an event to have had strong feelings about it. I have thought many times of how I felt the afternoon I heard about President Kennedy's death:

I had worked until very late the night before so I had not set my alarm and didn't wake up until around noon. I had a leisurely breakfast, read the morning paper, and dressed to go out—all without turning on the television or radio.

Just as I was leaving the house the gas man was arriving to read the meter. He greeted me with, "Terrible about the president, isn't it?

"What about him?" I asked.

"Somebody shot him and the governor of Texas," he answered.

The president and a governor! Our ever-present fear of the Russians sprang to my mind. Was this how they would attack us—by killing off our leaders? In a panic I rushed back into the house and turned on the television .

A newscaster was saying something about "President and Mrs. Johnson." President Johnson? We already had a new president!

I began to cry—not tears of grief for the president and his family, not tears left over from my panic, but tears of gratitude.

It suddenly occurred to me that before I even knew the president was dead a new president, whose orderly accession to the office had been provided for by the Constitution, had been sworn in. There had been no jockeying for power, no coup d'etat. The wheels of government had gone swiftly into motion and the terms of the Constitution had been fulfilled.

Ours, of course, is not the only country in the world that provides for the orderly replacement of its chief executive in case of an emergency, but many, many countries do not. I remember that in those few moments, standing alone in my living room with my hand on the television dial, I felt perhaps the strongest moment of pure patriotism that I have ever felt in my life.

I was especially delighted when a man in one of my classes turned out to be a survivor of D day. He wrote an engrossing account of his part in the Normandy invasion. When he was getting ready to put his book together, however, I began to worry a little bit about his D day story. Everyone in this class knew about D day, but how much would his younger readers know? Every now and then I mention something about World War II to someone in their twenties, or even their thirties, and I realize that they have only a hazy idea of what I am talking about.

Several years ago I interviewed Senator Margaret Chase Smith, former senator from Maine. At the time I interviewed her she was no longer in the Senate but was holding seminars on college campuses in which she discussed government affairs. I remember her saying to me, "I feel that it is important for students to have an opportunity to discuss vital issues with someone several generations their senior, someone who has lived through events which they haven't. You know, every twenty-five years there is a complete change in the youngsters who are coming out of high schools. Students today know nothing about World War II or Korea."

I began wondering whether the young people who read my student's book would realize the full significance of D day. I decided to conduct a survey. Actually I only surveyed one person—my niece, who is a junior in high school and a very bright, straight–A student. I asked her whether she knew what D day was. She thought a moment and then asked, "Wasn't it some kind of a big attack?"

What a blow an answer like that is to those of us who waited for months for the Allied invasion of Nazi occupied Europe and then waited breathlessly for news of friends and loved ones we thought might be in the invasion. What a blow for those who lost loved ones on the beaches of Normandy.

I suggested that my student write a little bit of background for his D day story. I told him how to do some superficial research which wouldn't take a lot of time but which would set the story in time and explain something of its significance. Here is his introduction to his D day story:

Tuesday, June 6, 1944, will be forever known as D day. It was the day the Allies of the free world invaded Nazi-occupied France in World War II. Nearly all of Western Europe had been occupied by Nazi Germany for four years. The people of the occupied countries were starving, being shipped in boxcars to forced labor and concentration camps in Germany, being shot as hostages, driven out of their homes, and more, by the Germans.

All of the radio and newsreel commentators (no TV then, of course) and all newspapers and magazines referred to Europe as "Fortress Europe." That's what it was. The Germans had turned the continent into a gigantic fortress and, all along any beaches that they thought the Allies might use for landing, they built what came to be called "The Atlantic Wall." Millions of tons of concrete had been poured by slave laborers to build pillboxes, bunkers, machine gun nests, and communications trenches on the cliffs overlooking the beaches. Concealed pipes ran to tanks of kerosene which were hidden in the cliffs. The mouths of the pipes opened into the grassy space between the beaches and the cliffs. All the Germans had to do was press a button and troops would be instantly burned alive. In the water on every beach steel and concrete obstacles were built just below high tide. There were obstacles of jagged triangles of steel, saw-toothed structures of iron, concrete cones, and wooden stakes with metal tips. Planted in among all of these barriers were thousands of mines. A touch would cause them to explode instantly. Stretched between the obstacles were massive entanglements of barbed wire.

The Allies designated five Normandy beaches as landing beaches and called them Omaha, Utah, Gold, Juno, and Sword. Omaha and Utah were invaded by American forces, Gold and Sword by the English, and Juno by the Canadians. Fighting with the three major Allies were companies of men who had escaped from the occupied countries of Europe.

Almost 5,000 ships carrying more than 200,000 soldiers, sailors, and coastguardsmen made up the invasion fleet. This is besides the hundreds of bombers, planes dropping paratroopers behind German lines, and planes and gliders that carried Allied airborne troops into Normandy behind the beaches.

I was in the second wave of infantry that landed on Omaha Beach. (His personal story of the landing followed.)

The man who wrote the above introduction read it to the class and there were several little gasps among class members as he described the size of the invasion force, the horror of the obstacle-strewn beaches on which the men had to land, and the general fortifications of the beaches. Every single member of the class remembered D day, but we had forgotten many details. If our memories of the invasion were fading, think how natural it is for young people born generations later to have no concept of it at all.

Remember, don't assume too much knowledge on the part of your readers. Every time you write a section of your book ask yourself,

"Have I included enough background material for my readers to understand how it really was?"

In his book *The Go-Betweens*, L. P. Hartley says, "The past is a foreign country." So it is, and it is the responsibility of those of us who write about the past to make sure our readers understand that country.

TWELVE

Religion

After sitting through several classes in which students read stories they had written about religion, I have concluded that the majority of American children in the late nineteenth and early twentieth centuries spent a good bit of their time being absolutely terrified of God. Story after story told of ministers who preached of sin, punishment, hell-fire, and damnation. Nearly all of the stories were funny to us as adults, but the pitiful, childish terror always showed through. I want to share a couple of these stories with you. One woman wrote:

One evening when I was a young girl, about nine or ten years old, I sat in the back seat of our Model A Ford as we bounced along bumpy, red clay roads through the foothills of the mountains of Georgia. We were on our way home from church. It had been a particularly strong sermon, laced with hell-fire and damnation—which was usually the case at our summer evening revival meetings.

I was in the midst of feeling my usual discontent for not being able to make that seemingly long walk down to the altar to surrender my life and to accept Jesus Christ as my personal Savior. I really wasn't quite certain what that meant, but I was feeling, keenly, the disappointment of my wonderful, Christian mother.

As we rode along I looked up into the sky and I was suddenly stricken with fear. The moon, a beautiful harvest moon, had suddenly taken on an orangish-red cast. A passage from Revelation sprang to my mind—that at the end of time, the moon would drip with blood. Merciful heavens! This was the end of the world and I wasn't ready!

That night made a lasting impression on me. It was many years before I could totally relinquish that fear and know in my heart that God is a loving, forgiving, and merciful father rather than a God of vengeance and wrath.

I often smile to myself when I see a full moon.

Another woman wrote of a similar experience. She, unlike the woman who wrote the preceding story, never came to see God as a loving father. Here is her very well told and amusing story:

One day, when I was about seven years old, my cousin and I were chasing each other wildly through the house. My mother told us that we should not run in the house, that if we wanted to play so recklessly we would have to go outside. Pretending that I hadn't heard my mother, I continued to chase my cousin, this time through the kitchen. I ran in front of my mother just as she was lifting a large kettle of jam from the stove, causing her to spill all of the jam and scald herself and the cat. Not a drop of jam fell on me.

I was conscience stricken. My mother told me I was a naughty, naughty girl and when my father came home from work he agreed.

That night we attended a revival service where the minister spent the whole evening talking about blood and the cross and the wicked burning in hell forever. I knew, of course, that he meant me. I shrank back in my seat and tried to be as little as possible.

It was summer and my mother made me a pallet on the floor of the living room because it was cooler there than in my bedroom. She left the door open and just hooked the screen to allow for the maximum amount of cool evening breeze.

I went to sleep with my wickedness and my probably horrible fate still on my mind. After sleeping uneasily for a little while I woke up. The moon was full and shining through the screen door. It had a cross on it! I sat straight up in bed, sure that this was an omen. The end of the world was coming and I wouldn't even get to wait until I was old and died before I was cast into hell—it would happen any minute! I started screaming and screaming at the top of my lungs.

Both my parents dashed into the living room to see what was the matter. I kept screaming, "The cross on the moon, the cross on the moon!"

My parents lit the lamp and then they both looked out the door and insisted that there was no cross on the moon. "Yes, there is!" I screamed, "Put out the light and you can see it!"

Finally, at my insistence, they blew out the lamp and my father got down on the floor beside me so I could show him the cross.

Suddenly, he began to laugh. "It's the cross frame in the middle of the screen door! Get down here, Eleanor, and have a look."

My mother got down on the floor with us and she began to laugh too. Papa opened the door to prove to me that with the screen door open the cross on the moon was gone.

When they asked why a cross on the moon had frightened me so, I sobbed my whole awful fears about being sent to hell because of the jam incident. They comforted me and said that while I had to learn to mind my mother I would have to be much, much more wicked than I had ever been before I would be sent to hell.

For the rest of the week, while the revival preacher was in town, I was sent to stay with the neighbors while my parents went to the meetings.

I don't know whether it was this incident or not— probably not—but somehow religion has never played an important part in my life. I have sometimes envied people to whom religion is important. Other times, I have felt annoyed when people have tried to foist their religion on me.

I like this story very much, partly because it is very funny, partly because it is written so well that I can just see that pitiful, sobbing little girl spilling out her fears. But I like it, too, because of the writer's frank statement at the end of the story about her adult feelings about religion.

I mentioned at the beginning of this chapter that I thought the American children in the late nineteenth and early twentieth centuries spent a good bit of their time being terrified of God. When I began teaching younger students, a woman in her early thirties wrote the following story which suggests that in some cases things haven't changed all that much:

When I think back on my Catholic upbringing, one important realization comes to mind. My behavior when it came to matters of religion was usually performed out of fear, not love, and that is why I do not go to church today. Then it seemed terrifying; now as I look back, only strange and amusing.

My sister, Phyllis, and I were forced to attend both church and Sunday school every Sunday, plus three weeks of Bible school in the summers. Phyllis was only twenty months older than I, so we usually did everything together, but our experiences were quite different. Phyllis looked at the world with a completely different attitude than I did. She was placid and matter-of-fact, and didn't question things, at least not as much as I did.

Like all good Catholic children, we were required to make our first holy communion when we were eight years old. Then our confirmation would be two years later. On the day before our first communion we were to make our first confession. Dressed all in white, with white veils and shoes, we felt as holy as saints, even though we had not yet performed a miracle.

We knew that at the confession the priest was to talk to us about our sins, and, believe me, we were taught one had to have sins. Only God and Jesus didn't. I was scared to death.

My greatest fear was the confessional booth itself. The booths were against the wall of the church, and they seemed very dark and glum to me. Each booth had three parts. The priest occupied the center part while in the parts on his right and left, with walls between them and the priest, were the sinners. One was supposed to pray to God and ask for forgiveness while the priest was hearing the person on the other side. There was a small window which slid open when the priest was ready to hear confessions. One could see only his head and shoulders.

All was dark. Even the cross in my part of the confessional scared me because with the darkness of the booth I could only see the shininess of the cross. I remember looking around hoping to see something else, but there was only Jesus on the cross and all that darkness. I wondered if the priest's booth was even darker.

The priest heard Phyllis's confession first, and kneeling in the booth, I listened to him as he mumbled to her in the other side of the booth. I could think of no sins. My mind was blank. Finally in desperation, I thought of something I could say, "I talked back to my mother this week." But wait—horror of horrors— I remembered something that had been taught to me in school. One sin was not enough. I needed at least two. How about, "I talked back to my mother two times this week"? No. That wouldn't do.

I was lost. My heart sank. I heard my sister's self-assured footsteps leaving the confessional booth. Of course she had done just fine, and here I was with not enough sins. My mind cast about in desperation. My eyes fell on the missal (a book containing all that is said in mass during the entire year) in my hands. I had it! The Ten Commandments would do just fine. I had learned them in summer Bible School. I learned that if you broke any one of these you would go to Hell, but could save yourself if you confessed. Now I felt more confident. If only I could remember one, no two, commandments without stumbling.

The priest slid open the small window to his part of the booth. I could see only his shadow and a cross on the wall and hear his strong voice whisper, "Go ahead."

I began: "Bless me, Father, for I have sinned. This is my first confession. I talked back to my mom one time. I committed adultery twice, and I coveted my neighbor's wife two times."

(SILENCE)

Finally, the priest said to the little eight-year-old girl, "For your penance, child, I want you to go home and ask your mother to teach you how to say a proper confession." I could tell from the tone of his voice that he was gravely displeased. Obviously, the Ten Commandments had been a bad idea.

I told my mother what the priest had said. She seemed bemused about the penance. When I told her about my sins, she said, "Daisy Etta, those sins are only for adults!" She didn't tell me why but I assumed I needed something a bit more simple. So, as a result, during the next few years, I confessed many thefts of bubble gum that I never stole, admitted using God's name in vain many times although I never swore, and claimed to have missed a lot of church when I was actually there every Sunday. All of these lies for the priest's benefit and the salvation of my soul.

Each class produces one or more inspiring stories of answered prayer when we work on the assignment on religion. I love these stories and wish I could share all of them with you. That, of course, is impossible, but I wanted very much to share at least one. I read my file of stories about prayer over and over, trying to decide which one I should include. All were wonderful.

Finally, after a great deal of soul searching, I decided to use one of my own—not because it is more inspiring than the others but because it was published in *Weekly Unity*.

I have always taught this course with the idea that the stories written by the class were intended for families and friends, particularly for future generations, and not for publication. However, someone in nearly every class asks about publishing. I imagine some of my readers are also thinking about the possibility of trying to publish all or part of their autobiographies. I am, therefore, including this story and telling you how I constructed it for publication (see chapter 30 for more details). I hope this information will help you in case you want to prepare one or more of your stories for submission to an editor.

I am inserting the story here because, since it is on the subject of religion, it belongs in this chapter.

Here is my story:

If I hadn't been in very great need about a year ago, I might never have grasped the full significance of what has become one of my favorite Biblical passages. More important, I might never have known so surely the depth of God's concern for our practical, everyday needs.

An amusement park in South Missouri, which might be called a "Disneyland of the Ozarks," had hired me to do a writing assignment. The park is a complete 1880 village with an atmosphere of quiet, nostalgic charm combined with Ozark hillbilly hijinks. Throughout the day, at various points in the park, actors and actresses perform short plays, five to seven minutes in length. My assignment was to rewrite, sharpen, and improve twelve of the scripts already in use and to write four completely new ones.

It was a particularly difficult kind of writing. Each of these very short plays had to have a complete plot. They had to be based on hillbilly humor, which was completely new to me. They had to have both dialogue and vaudeville-type "sight gags," and they had to be funny enough to cause people to stand in the blazing Ozark sun to watch them.

I tackled the rewrites with enthusiasm. Before long, my typewriter was spelling "get" with an "i" instead of an "e," dropping its g's and saying "Ah" instead of "I," and I was having lots of fun. But as I neared the end of the rewrite part of the assignment, a feeling of uneasiness began to steal over me. Soon I would have to start on the original scripts, and I didn't know what I was going to write about. In spite of the fact that I had been studying comedy writing and Ozark lore for weeks, I didn't have a single idea.

By the time I typed the final rewrite script, I was in a state of panic. The next day I would have to start writing the new scripts, and my deadline was just two weeks away. Still no ideas! I lay awake most of that night worrying and searching every corner of my brain for just the beginnings of a plot.

While I was eating breakfast the next morning, I suddenly remembered once hearing a minister say that when one is facing a dilemma it is a good idea to open the Bible at random, and sometimes the book will automatically open to a page that will provide an answer to the dilemma. At the time I thought the minister was talking nonsense. Still, I was completely sunk and anything seemed worth a try. Without really expecting to find anything helpful, I picked up the Bible. I opened it to one page—nothing that helped. I opened it a second time—still nothing. I opened it a third time—this time to the twenty-first chapter of John.

The chapter tells of Jesus appearing on the beach at the Sea of Tiberias after his resurrection. He called to His disciples who were fishing in a boat offshore, and asked if they were catching anything. The disciples called back that they were not. Jesus answered, "Shoot the net to starboard, and you will make a catch."

The disciples followed His instruction, and within seconds their net was so full of fish they could scarcely haul it aboard. Immediately, they realized that the man on the beach must be Jesus and they rushed to greet Him.

When they arrived on the beach, Jesus had a fire going and was roasting fish and bread over a charcoal fire. "Come and have breakfast," He called.

As I finished reading the passage, it was as if someone had turned on a light in my head. I had one of those moments of illumination when the Spirit teaches us more in seconds than we could learn in a lifetime of living. I knew the passage was intended for me at that moment. I knew that although there had been other times when Jesus had provided food in more spectacular ways—multiplying a little basket of loaves and fishes to feed the multitude, turning water into wine—this particular story of Jesus the Provider was unique.

The earlier stories of Jesus miraculously providing food and drink had occurred before his resurrection, when He was still in His human state. This incident occurred after His resurrection, when He no longer had physical needs Himself. It demonstrated to me that His translation from the physical state did not lift Him above an interest in the physical needs of His friends. He had only a few short days on earth before He was to make His final departure. Yet part of that precious time He spent helping His disciples improve their financial condition by

telling them where to fish; and part of the time He spent caring for their physical needs by preparing breakfast for them.

The story told me that God is vitally interested in our everyday problems. (After all, what is more mundane than preparing
breakfast?) I knew He would help me write my plays. Writing
them was my job, part of my means of earning a living. I closed
my eyes and said, "Father, You know I have this job to do and
You know I need Your help. I'm sure You didn't give me the job
so I could fail at it, so please help me."

I decided that having offered this prayer I would stop worrying and assume that my answer was on its way. I began washing
the breakfast dishes, occupying my thoughts with what I was
going to fix for dinner that night. Suddenly, there came rushing
into my head, crowding out all thought of dinner menus, the
entire script for a play, with all characters and dialogue intact.
When this play was performed, it ran about seven minutes, so
it seems logical that it should have taken at least that long for
its dialogue to run through my mind. It didn't though; I had it
all in a second or two.

I almost ran to my typewriter. I sat down and wrote the entire script without stopping. I retyped it once the next day,
changing only a word or a punctuation mark here and there,
and it was finished. God had done my work for me. Not only
that, He had done it superbly. The script had exactly the zany
humor and hillbilly flavor it needed but it also had a grace and
charm that I would never have dreamed possible in that kind of
a script.

Of course, I still had three plays to go and still no ideas, but
I knew the ideas would come. My panic was gone, leaving my
mind free for an inflow of ideas. I sat down at my desk saying to
myself, "I don't have to wait for His help. God is helping me
now." I wrote those three scripts in much the same way I would
write anything else, with ideas coming in bits and pieces, with
lots of rewriting, rearranging, and polishing, but I was always
confident that God was helping me. I met my deadline and the
people at the park were delighted with the plays.

I believe that God gives us the particular soul adventure we need at each stage of our development. He taught me through that incident that He is willing, even eager, to help us meet the most practical needs of our everyday lives if we will ask for His help and have faith that He will give it.

Do you have a soul adventure to share with your descendants? If you do, by all means include it in your book. There may be times, many years from now, when your descendants reading your autobiography will come upon it unexpectedly just when they, themselves, are needing a spiritual lift. What a wonderful link across the generations that would be.

Maybe your religious story is a funny one, like those of the little girls who were scared out of their wits by revival preachers and a full moon. Even if your religion story is a bitter one, write it anyway if you feel like it. Or maybe you have funny, inspirational, *and* bitter stories about religion. Lots of people do. Maybe you will want to include many facets of your religious life. Maybe you won't. It's up to you, but give it some thought.

Sometimes I have students who just don't have anything to say about religion and that's fine too. Their books are filled with other things.

THIRTEEN

Relatives

A grandmother wrote the following story about her five-year-old granddaughter:

I always tried to keep supplies on hand so that when Christy came to visit I could give her an ice cream cone. One day her mother dropped her off at my house unexpectedly and I was out of both cones and ice cream. After she had played around the house for a few minutes Christy came into the kitchen where I was working and said, "Grandmother, can I have an ice cream cone?"

I said, "Honey, I'm sorry but I don't have any ice cream cones today."

She stood there looking both surprised and disappointed for a few seconds and said, in what sounded to me like a rather accusing tone, "Well, I thought you always had ice cream cones."

I confess I love the role of indulgent grandmother and I guess the miffed note in Christy's voice rather put me on the defensive. I said, "Well, Christy, I'll bet your mother doesn't have ice cream cones for you every time you ask for them."

"No, she doesn't," answered Christy, "but she isn't my grandmother!"

Without realizing it Christy had made a profound observation; that is, a very special relationship sometimes exists between grandparents and grandchildren. Special relationships often exist between other family members as well. Sometimes they are happy, constructive relationships, and sometimes they are unhappy and destructive. Do you have, or have you had, special relationships with brothers or sisters, aunts, uncles, cousins, nieces, nephews, or grandchildren? If so, be sure to write about them.

The following story tells about a little girl's relationship with her uncle. The writer of the story took considerable pains to be honest about her present feelings for her uncle. This required several days of dredging up and having a good look at emotions which she had kept hidden from herself for years. Her almost fierce determination to be honest makes this story an exceptional example of the kind of illuminating hindsight that makes for superior autobiographies. Before you read her story I suggest that you reread ground rule number three—Be honest.

Family gatherings were fairly constant happenings when I was small. Being born into a large Italian clan meant one would never be just with parents on Christmas, New Year's Day, and Thanksgiving, for example. The whole family always got together at my Uncle Tom's. Not only did we gather at Uncle Tom's on holidays, but we also visited him and my Aunt Louise once a month.

Uncle Tom was next to the oldest of my father's nine brothers, my father being the baby of the family. My father looked up to his older brother and these visits were happy occasions for him. Dad had been a shy little boy and Uncle Tom often had to step in and protect him from other boys. I think this is why my father felt so content when he was around Uncle Tom.

Christmas mornings were especially memorable for me. My older brother and I opened our presents with Mom and Dad and then quickly drove to Uncle Tom's and Aunt Louise's house where all the family met. Some of my father's brothers and their families had moved away from Chicago, but even the out-of-towners would be sure to come to Uncle Tom's for Christmas. All of my uncles were married and eight of them had a large family of children. There were always at least sixty people when the family got together at Uncle Tom's.

Uncle Tom had only one grown son, the smallest family of all the brothers, so he didn't need a lot of space for his own family. But having his extended family visit meant more to him than anything. He considered family gatherings so important that he built a new house with a huge recreation room the size of a ballroom to accommodate his family. There was always plenty to do at the family gathering. Uncle Tom had ping pong, pool tables, and eight slot machines—penny, nickel, dime, and quarter. We children would play the slots until our fingers were numb. My uncle didn't make any money on the machines when we played because he always gave us the change to operate them.

I can remember when I was little how Uncle Tom would boast, politely of course, about the bountiful food and drink. There were always trays of meat fit for a queen laid out—the best brisket, ham, and breaded veal one could imagine. The cheeses were of the finest quality—provolone, mozzarella, Swiss, and plenty of yellow American for the kids who didn't appreciate the more exotic cheeses.

My Aunt Louise always had her maid come the day before we all arrived to help cook spaghetti and meatballs with plenty of Italian sausage to flavor the sauces. Aunt Louise bought this sausage at a little Italian store where it was made daily from the finest ingredients. Uncle Tom would watch everyone, making sure they ate enough, saying, "Eat more. There's plenty!" He wanted to make sure everyone had a good time. And we did— we had a wonderful time. All day long we ate, played, talked, and fussed over some new baby cousin.

As I began growing up I gradually became aware of monetary value. I knew my father didn't make a great deal of money because our house was very modest, and so was our family car. I also knew that the meats my mother served were not the same quality as Uncle Tom's and Aunt Louise's. I guess I was about eight when I started questioning the fact that Uncle Tom's diamond tie tacks, his lizard skin shoes, and silk suits must have cost a great deal of money, not to mention the elaborate house with all the great food.

I remember that one evening as we were driving home from a family party I asked my parents where Uncle Tom worked. The reason I didn't ask Uncle Tom himself this question was because you just didn't ask Uncle Tom questions. Everyone loved and respected him in a rather awesome way. He was the one who asked the questions.

My parents never answered me directly about my uncle's job. They always just said something on the order of "We don't need to know where everyone works," and "Children should be seen and not heard." That was all the answer I got. As I got a little older I came to realize, with the help of a few cousins and also because of rumors, that my wonderful, good-hearted uncle was a big man in the Mafia. My older brother and I watched a weekly television show called *The Untouchables*, which was about the mob, and my brother told me the things those men were doing were the things my Uncle Tom was doing.

When my brother explained the Mafia to me he said that these men worked in the underground. I took everything very literally as a child and thought my uncle went underground to work. Why, I wondered, did he have to work in such a dark, dark place? I believe the reason I was so naive and took all of these things so literally was because answers to my questions were always so very vague.

As I grew older I began to realize what "underground" really meant. I felt that all the men in *The Untouchables* were wicked, but I could never relate them to my uncle, no matter what my brother said. Uncle Tom, in my eyes, was not capable of violence. Even though as a teenager I saw him get dressed up late at night and go out with strange looking men, I never questioned his actions. Nor can I deny the fact that he never showed me any side of himself other than the domestic uncle. One of my last memories of him, for example, was his last Christmas when he was dying of cancer. He was walking around his recreation room in extreme pain making sure that everyone had a good time.

But during many hours of struggle I have begun to sort out my feelings. I realize now that the result of forcing children to suppress thoughts, feelings, and questions can have an insidious and inhibiting effect on them and prevent them from ever really knowing what they feel. I was never allowed to ask questions about Uncle Tom. If I did, the answer was always abrupt and vague. Even when seeing movies about the mob I was told silently that questions were not to be asked. I was told crime was bad but at the same time I knew I was expected to suppress all of my questions about Uncle Tom and have the same admiration for him that my parents had.

At the age of forty, when I am no longer told how to feel, I can choose my own values and discriminate according to those values. That is the essence of age. I own myself and that entitles me to choose my own feelings. I am using this freedom to ask myself how I feel about my Uncle Tom. I no longer see him as a hero. Instead, I see a man with an enormous ego. I don't necessarily feel ego is bad and I'm still grateful to him for all the lovely holidays, dinners, and so on. The difference now is that I can allow myself to admit that he lived a life of crime even though he did keep it departmentalized from his family life. Uncle Tom wasn't the completely wonderful man I thought him to be when I was a child. My questions about him aren't all answered yet, but I believe he must have been a person who somehow thought he had to buy love, a person as repressed as I was. Was he an example of repression of self-honesty, an example of departmentalizing one's thinking and feelings carried to an extreme?

A young woman at a community college in Chicago wrote the following story about another special family relationship:

I experienced death for the first time at the age of ten. I had a baby brother named Zachary who would have been two years old the year that he died. Zachary was a sweet and lovable child with bright laughing eyes. His hair was soft black and curly like lamb's wool. He had beautiful, immaculate skin, just like the day he was born into the world.

Zachary was the favorite child in our family because there hadn't been a baby in our household for eight years. The years before Zachary was born, my brother, sister, and I would always ask our parents if we could have a baby brother or sister for Christmas. My parents' reply would be, "If you're real good, this year, Santa Claus will bring you one." Each year until Zachary was born, my brother, sister, and I looked for a baby underneath the tree on Christmas. We were disappointed when we did not find a baby there, thinking that Santa Claus was angry at us for doing something bad.

One day in December my mother went to the hospital. She came home a few days later with Zachary. My family was overjoyed. My mother said, "Santa Claus brought one of your presents early this year." We all laughed and gazed at the beautiful bundle we had longed for for so long. He had such bright eyes and his face was so perfect and round. He greedily sucked on the nipple of his baby bottle.

The day before Zachary died, my whole family was at the park. It was a beautiful, hot, and sunny day. Zachary and I were sliding on the sliding boards and swinging in the swings. My brother Charles and sister Nancy were also in on the fun. We took turns chasing each other up the sliding boards. One of us would always wait at the bottom to catch hold of Zachary before he landed on the ground.

Suddenly it started to rain. My mother yelled, "Time to go home. Get into the car." We all got into the automobile and went home with our parents. That ended our day because it continued to rain for the rest of the evening and we couldn't go outside. This was the very last day I got to enjoy my baby brother Zachary.

The following day, my parents got up to go to the supermarket to buy some groceries. They reminded us not to let anyone into the house while they were gone. My oldest sister was babysitting Zachary, Charles, and me. Zachary was lying on the bed in the bedroom, asleep. Charles, Nancy, and I were watching cartoons on television. Suddenly Zachary started gasping for breath as though he were choking. My sister jumped from the floor where she was sitting, grabbed Zachary, and started patting him on the back. By this time, we had all surrounded the bed. My sister shouted nervously, "Go get Mrs. Ann. Go get Mrs. Ann!"

I ran across the hall to get Mrs. Ann, our next door neighbor. I bammed on the door and Mrs. Ann opened it, asking me what was the matter. I said, "Zachary is choking; he can't catch his breath!" Mrs. Ann came quickly behind me into the bedroom to see the baby. Zachary had stopped gasping. Mrs. Ann felt his pulse and said, "I think we should call an ambulance."

I started crying and so did my sister and brother. Zachary had been in the hospital several times before with pneumonia, and we didn't want him to go back this time and leave us. We did not know that this was going to be his last departure. I started rubbing his arm. I held my baby brother Zachary's hand; it felt a little cool. I bent down and kissed him on the lips. I had a funny feeling that something was going to happen. I couldn't figure out what.

The ambulance came and they took my baby brother to the hospital. The next door neighbor, Mrs. Ann, went along with Zachary and the drivers. About twenty minutes later, although it seemed like time was standing still, Mrs. Ann phoned and asked were our parents home. I noticed the hoarseness in her voice, as if she had been crying. My heart dropped into my stomach as I asked how Zachary was. She replied, "He's all right." I told her my parents were not home yet. Mrs. Ann wanted me to tell them as soon as they came home to go to Jackson Park Hospital. Relief touched my heart thinking that my baby brother was all right.

Five minutes later my parents walked in with bags of groceries. My sister and I explained to them what had happened. My mother started crying and they both left quickly to go to the hospital.

Finally they returned home. My mother came through the door crying. I asked her, "Where is Zachary?"

My mother said, "Zachary has left us. He's gone."

A great, great sadness struck my heart. It was like a wound from a knife. I looked around the room and my sister had fainted. My brother Charles was crying, and I started crying, too. My father was looking real sad. He tried to embrace us all at the same time.

It was the very first time I had experienced death in my family. It seemed like my whole world had come to an end. While writing this paper, I am in tears.

I have read this story at least half a dozen times and each time I am in tears by the time I finish reading. The last sentence tells why the writer is able to move me to tears again and again. She says, "While I am writing this paper, I am in tears."

This sentence is important to us in autobiographical writing. The reason her story causes the reader to identify so completely with the writer's sorrow is that she allowed herself, while writing, to experience again the grief she felt when her little brother died. Sometimes it costs us something emotionally to relive painful experiences, but summon the courage to write about your sad times as well as your happy times. Have the courage, too, to let your emotions well up even if it causes you to shed a tear or two.

I want to issue one word of caution about something which may occur when you write about your family. You may find that when other members of your family read what you have written, their memories will differ from yours. This occurred once in my own family when my sister, Lillian, wrote the following story about our cousin's imaginary playmate. Incidentally, notice that when she mentions Bill she identifies him specifically in parentheses after his name. This is a good idea because it may sometime help some member of your family who is trying to figure out something about ancestors.

Our cousin, Bill Gould (son of Herbert and Bertie Gould), often came to spend the day with us. He was probably about five when this episode occurred. My sister, Carol, would have been about eight and I would have been seven.

Bill always took Little Midget with him everywhere he went. Now, Little Midget was visible only to Bill but everyone in the family was aware of her presence because Bill talked to her all the time. She was always by his side. He lifted her up onto a chair at the table, fed her from a plate that he insisted be set for her, and was very good to her at all times.

On this particular occasion Bill, Carol, and I went across the street from our house to our grandparents' (the Goulds) house. Of course Little Midget went with us. A big trunk always stood in the front hall of the house, and a favorite pastime of ours was to climb up and slide off the trunk's rounded top. On this occasion, as Carol, Bill, and I were climbing up onto the trunk, Bill began to cry.

We asked what was the matter and he said, "You have taken up all the room and there is no room for Little Midget!"

We "scooted" over and tried to be small, but still there was no room for Little Midget. We finally saw that Bill wasn't going to stop crying until one of us got off of the trunk. Carol said I had to be the one to get down because she was the oldest. I was furious but Carol was firm and Bill was fiercely protecting Little Midget.

Of course, all I could see on the trunk was an empty space, but Bill carefully lifted Little Midget up and got her settled in my place. So I had to stand and watch while Carol and Bill had fun sliding off the trunk, one on each side of my empty place.

Lillian read this story aloud to my sisters, Carol, Naomi, and me. After she had finished reading Naomi asked, "Well, where was I?"

Lillian answered, "I don't know. I guess you weren't born yet."

Naomi said, "Well, of course I was born, I'm older than Bill!"

"Oh, that's right, you are," Lillian agreed. "Well, I don't know but you weren't there. It was just Carol and me."

"Well," said Naomi, somewhat huffily, "I may not have been there on that particular day, but I certainly played with Little Midget on the trunk."

Suddenly, both Naomi and Lillian began to laugh. "Do you realize," asked Naomi, her eyes getting teary from laughter, "that we are arguing about someone who never existed?"

Lillian turned to me, looking both amused and chagrined, and said, "For goodness sake, don't put this in your book. People will think you belong to a family of lunatics."

Incidentally, I might add that Bill had sent Little Midget wherever children send their imaginary playmates when they outgrow them more than fifteen years before I was born. However, I have heard about Little Midget all of my life. In fact, I know more about her than I do about some of my real relatives.

Unfortunately, disputes over memories about families aren't always funny. The advice I have to offer is to be ready to listen if other members of your family disagree with you. They might be right and you might be wrong. Give yourself a little time to think about their memory of an event or a situation. Ask them as many questions about it as you can think of—all in the friendliest possible spirit, of course. Try to dig up related memories to help you or ask a third party for his or her memory of the situation.

Always bear in mind that important as our memoirs are, they are not as important as family unity. Rather than have a major family dispute—which nearly occurred in the family of one of my students—it would be better to leave the controversial incident out of your story. Another possible solution would be to write your own memory of the situation and then add that "so and so" remembers it somewhat differently, describing the differences.

FOURTEEN

Courtship

Only once have a husband and wife attended one of my classes together. It seems that in most families one spouse or the other assumes the role of chronicler. The class always enjoyed hearing the stories Blanche and Cecil Carstenson wrote independently about the same situation.

This is something you might want to think about. It would add interest to your book if you could persuade your spouse—or sister, brother, or any other family member, or friend—to write a chapter about something you both experienced. Even someone who doesn't want to write the entire story of his or her life might be persuaded to write a chapter or two. This could also be a way of settling the kind of family dispute that arose between my sisters in the previous chapter. If someone disagrees with you about something you are writing, invite them to write their own chapter on the same subject and include it in the book. Even if there is no dispute, though, no two people have exactly the same experience in a given situation.

Before sharing Blanche's and Cecil's stories about their courtship, I want to tell you a little bit about them. I think you will be interested, as I was, in contrasting their early years with their later years.

Blanche and Cecil are the only members of any of my classes that I had met before they came to class. I first met them when I was writing an article about the many artists who live in Westport, an historic district of Kansas City, Missouri. They have since become dear friends. Both Cecil and Blanche, who are in their seventies, are artists with national reputations.

Cecil has sold nearly two thousand pieces of wood sculpture. His work is owned by private collectors in forty states and more than twenty-five museums and public buildings throughout the country own and display his work. One of his pieces was featured in the Missouri building at the 1964 New York World's Fair. His book, *Craft and Creation of Wood Sculpture*, was published by Charles Scribner's Sons in 1971 and will soon be reissued in paperback.

Blanche's textile collages and batik wall hangings and banners have also been displayed in prestigious galleries in many parts of the country. Her designs and techniques have been included in six books on textile art. She has received major commissions from churches, colleges, libraries, historical societies, and individuals.

The Carstensons met and were married in their hometown of Marquette, Kansas. "I was interested in sculpture even then," said Cecil, "but of course I had to make a living for my family so I got a job as a telephone installer for Western Electric. I was with Western until I was fifty-five, but for a long time before I retired I was sculpting forty hours a week. You can find time to do anything you really want to do, you know."

"Cecil had to support the family and I had to take care of him and our two children," said Blanche. "We had very little free time in those early days when our children were young, but one day I saw a design for a wall hanging in a women's magazine and I thought, 'I believe I could do that.' I saved the design and kept looking at it for a long time before I was finally able to get to work. I took classes whenever I could, usually in design. I wouldn't take anything for the family years or for the art years or for the years when I was able, to some extent, to combine the two."

A tour of their beautiful home is like touring a fine gallery with two well-informed, enthusiastic guides. Every room, hall, and stairwell is filled with their own art work and the art work of their friends and students. Reading their stories of their courtship came as quite a jolt to me after having met them originally in what can only be described as an exceptionally gracious, prosperous, and artistic setting.

Here is Blanche's courtship story:

The year I was fifteen and in the second year of high school my parents bought a small farm near Marquette, Kansas, a town of seven hundred people. My family started attending the Methodist church and I joined the youth group and began singing in the choir.

I enjoyed high school. I made some girl friends at school and at church but I had no special friends among the boys and had no dates with any of them. Not having dates like the other girls was a great disappointment to me. It also made it very difficult for me to go to school and church affairs. I was embarrassed to have to have my father or younger brother take me places.

The spring I was sixteen, while singing in the choir one Sunday, I noticed a new boy in the back row of the church. He kept his eyes on me all during the service. Of course, I asked who this dark-eyed, intense young man was. I learned that he was Cecil Carstenson, that his family lived on a farm, and that he did not go to high school. Since high school was so important in my life, I just knew this boy did not have much ambition.

In a couple of weeks, Cecil got courage and asked my father if he could take me home from church. His asking my father's permission indicated to me that he was very old-fashioned, even laughable. My parents thought he had very good manners. I accepted his invitation but those short journeys did not change my mind about him. He invited me to some other affairs; sometimes I would accept and sometimes I turned him down in unkind ways.

I was, as I think most young girls are, very insecure. I did not know if people liked me or whether I was pretty. When I asked my mother if I were pretty, she would say I was pretty enough. I thought only of myself. I certainly did not consider the great difficulty Cecil had in getting permission to use his family's Model T Ford. He usually had to beg the family to wait in town after church while he took me home, as they could not go home until he returned the car. I also failed to appreciate the sacrifice he must have made to buy even an ice cream soda at the drugstore.

But having such a persistent suitor gave me personal power for the first time. He was awkward and socially unskilled and lacked confidence because of his lack of high school experience. I'm afraid I enjoyed making him so uncomfortable that he would stand on one foot and stammer his desire to take me someplace. He sent me a flowery Valentine and bought me a box of chocolates. Although I had never had a box of chocolates, I disdained to accept the gift.

Even though Cecil was the only boy who really asked me for a date, I continued to mistreat him for more than two years. Occasionally I would go someplace with him but I was never very nice to him. I was dreaming of a handsome, tall, sophisticated, brilliant, and rich young man who would come and sweep me away into some great new life. Or perhaps one of the football heroes of our school would notice me. My parents were disgusted with my behavior. Here I had a chance with a boy of a good family, a boy whose family had some rich farmland and some prospects, and I did not accept my good fortune.

I graduated from high school and passed examinations which qualified me to teach in a country school. I sent out many applications but did not get a school that year. I longed to go to college but did not have the money. There were no jobs in our small town and girls did not go off by themselves to a city in those days. I was stuck at home, a most unhappy girl. I helped with the farm work such as shocking wheat in summer and husking corn in the fall. I took a job as a "hired girl" helping a pregnant neighbor woman until her baby was born.

I finally faced the fact that no romantic knight was going to come on a white horse to carry me away and decided I had better face reality and take an interest in those around me.

I heard that Cecil was going to Kansas City to attend an engineering school. Now that was interesting and it might be nice to have someone to write to in Kansas City. I somehow got Cecil's sister to invite me to their home after church one Sunday before he left for school. That day I was just as "nice as pie." I laughed at Cecil's jokes and asked him to write to me. When he took me home that evening, I even let him kiss me.

We exchanged letters during his short course in engineering school and at the end of the course, he came home to see me instead of taking a job in Kansas City as he had intended. He worked in Marquette that summer and saved money so he could go back to school in the fall. We spent a lot of time talking that summer. I discovered that here was a young man who had ambition and determination to do something worthwhile. I learned that he had not been allowed to go to high school because his father hated farming and forced Cecil to do the work. I also learned that he had studied algebra, geometry, and trigonometry from books loaned to him by the town's newspaper editor and consequently, he had been allowed to skip those subjects in the engineering school.

Cecil developed an interest in music because of my love for it and at Easter, he took me to hear Handel's "Messiah" sung by the renowned choral group at Lindsborg, Kansas. For both of us, this was our introduction to great music. Cecil also took me to hear the world famous singer Madame Shumann Heink during the Easter festival. We gradually began to realize that we were in love.

Fall came and Cecil went back to school. I got a teaching position at a country school near home and I loved teaching the fifteen children. Cecil wrote to me from school and soon asked me to marry him and I accepted.

We were married the week after my teaching job ended in May, 1927. I have loved this wonderful, kind man all these fifty-four years. I have really tried to make up for my early mistreatment of him and have tried to help him realize his dreams as he has helped me realize many of mine. We reared two fine children and have had a happy life together.

Blanche's story is a wonderful demonstration of ground rule number three—Be Honest. She not only admits that she was a rude, selfish, and opportunistic girl, she also admits that she was never popular with boys and young men. In fact, she entitled this story about her courtship "My Only Suitor."

In fairness to Blanche I should add that although the class agreed that she certainly was mean to Cecil they also agreed that she was only partially to blame. For centuries society has inflicted the "romantic knight" syndrome on young women, which was not only unfair to them but also to young men. I have noticed that when younger people in my classes have written about their courtships they seem to have had a more realistic approach to finding a mate.

Cecil's story about the courtship substantiates Blanche's story. She didn't make it easy! In fact, reading his story will show you just how hard she made it for him. However, the great value that he places on the successful conclusion of that courtship is indicated by the fact that he wrote about it when the assignment was "The Accomplishment of Which You Are Most Proud."

My most important accomplishment was the most difficult and was one that had to be made before I could accomplish much of anything. Stating the problem simply it was the need to change my state of mind—to get from "here" to "there."

"Here" was where I found myself in my late teens and early twenties and "there" was when I had eliminated the terrible obstacle of feeling very inferior, almost an untouchable. I had been told that I must "make something of myself" but I felt inadequate. This was caused primarily by my not getting to go to high school where I thought everyone learned everything. I was sure that after high school people had no problems. They knew how to talk and act and dress, and so on.

I thought bumpkin, clodhopper, slob, and ignorant country boy who knew nothing but how to work, were written all over me in scarlet letters. To make matters worse, I was overweight and felt that everyone saw me as the fat boy. All this plus being part of a small minority of non-Swedish in a predominantly Swedish community, where it was considered superior to be a Swede. Self-pity accompanied my feelings of inferiority.

While having to overcome the obstacle of feeling totally inferior, I had to first overcome another most difficult obstacle. I had my eye on a beautiful young lady sitting in the front row of the choir. I decided that was the girl I was going to marry, or at least get to know and then decide, depending upon her wishes. Her name was Blanche Williams and it turned out that she had not only gone to high school, she was about to become a teacher.

Blanche turned out to be a "tough nut to crack"; quite naturally she had nothing but disdain for this uncouth, uneducated, fat boy with no manners, and more. At a later date Blanche admitted that she got a sadistic pleasure out of seeing me grovel at her feet. From my very limited resources I bought her gifts, which I could ill afford, only to have them rejected.

I include winning Blanche in this "accomplishment of which I am most proud" assignment because it was a necessary step toward gaining some self respect and getting rid of my deep feeling of inferiority. After this accomplishment, which was "uphill all the way," all other accomplishments were relatively anti-climactic. I will list a few other accomplishments that I am also proud of but which would never have been possible if I had not changed my attitude from a negative one to a positive one.

Blanche was stubborn, but I was even more stubborn and when she said "yes" I was on my way. From then on the accomplishments were not my accomplishments, but our

accomplishments. I got the credit as it was in the male chauvin-
istic Dark Ages era.

Cecil then goes on to say that he was proud of the fact that (his
lack of high school notwithstanding!) he taught sculpture in one
university and lectured or conducted workshops in nine other uni-
versities; that Charles Scribner's Sons published his book; that he
was a member of the Committee on Art for the Ford Foundation;
that he is listed in *Who's Who in American Art* and in the Midwest
section of *Who's Who in America*; that as a Lieutenant Colonel in the
Air Force in World War II he was awarded the Legion of Merit; that
although he had 1,100 men under his command not one of them
ever had to be court-martialed; that in three court-martials he was
charged with insubordination (he was cleared all three times); that
he rose from a telephone installer to a high management position in
the Western Electric Company; and that although he had 158 employees not one was fired. (Incidentally, I know that Cecil has many
more achievements to his credit but I have listed enough to give you
an idea of the importance he placed on his successful courtship.) He
finishes his story:

In conclusion I want to stress that none of these accomplishments would have been possible if I had not first erased my
defeatism and feeling of being totally inferior and if I had not
married the right woman.

Cecil's story of how the scared little country boy got from his
terrible "here" to his wonderful "there" by developing a positive attitude has been a great inspiration to me since the first time I read it.

Cecil had a wonderful idea, which I will pass on to you. His son
and daughter both live in other cities and it has been his habit to

write to them once a week. While the classes were in session (he and Blanche attended either two or three semesters) instead of writing his usual we-did-this-or-we-did-that-this-week-letters, he wrote one of his stories as his weekly letter.

Aleon DeVore, coordinator of the Rocky Mountain Writers Guild Senior Writing Competition, had a similar, though different idea, which you might like to try. Once a week she sends her little grand-daughter, Laura, what Aleon calls a "granny letter." The letters are short and informally written and each one tells a story from Aleon's life.

"I don't know how interested she is in receiving the letters but I always put a quarter in to make sure she opens them," said Aleon, laughing at her own deviousness. "Also, I asked my daughter to have Laura read them aloud to her. She's very proud of being able to read and it's a way to make sure she knows what is in them. My feeling is that sometimes she will be very interested in the stories and some-times she won't be at all interested, but at least she will read them once and perhaps think about them from time to time and probably really value them when she is older. Her mother is saving all of them for her."

When other grandparents think they might like to try this idea Aleon always tells them, "Don't expect an answer, no preaching, no self-pity, and no begging, just stories that you hope will be fun for a child to read." Aleon added that after the first couple of letters she asked her daughter to point out flaws in her letters—things Laura didn't understand, and so on.

I think Cecil's and Aleon's ideas are wonderful. The letters can become chapters in your book and meanwhile you will have an audi-ence and give pleasure to members of your family who may be in a distant city.

Turning
Points

We all have several major turning points in our lives—graduation from high school, from college, getting married, having
children, maybe getting divorced, getting our first job, losing a job,
changing careers, perhaps even immigrating to a new country. However, many of us, perhaps all of us, have other turning points which
are more subtle, but which are as significant as some of the obvious
ones mentioned above. These turning points may be changes in ourselves—the discovery of a new way of looking at things or of a new
way to live; or they may be brought about by some unusual circumstances outside ourselves.

As you read this chapter, give some thought to possible turning
points in your own life. Often we don't realize we have passed a turning point while we are living through it. We need the perspective of
a backward glance in order to recognize it.

The first turning point story that I want to share with you was
written by a thirty-eight-year-old woman who made a discovery
which she calls "pure gold."

She had married her high school sweetheart the summer after
graduation. That was in the late 1950s, when the majority of young

women still thought their own real future lay in marrying the right man. She was one of many thousands of American women who skipped college herself, got a job, and put her husband through college. She worked as a receptionist in a doctor's office until her husband was well established in a career. When they decided to start a family she had two miscarriages, and after the second one her doctor advised her not to try again to have children. Here is her story:

The day after my thirtieth birthday, when we had been married nearly twelve years, Tom told me he wanted a divorce because he wanted to marry someone else. I was stunned and desperate. I tried everything I could think of to recapture his interest. I dieted until I was so skinny people hardly recognized me. I dyed my hair and bought new, "sexy" looking clothes which I now realize probably made me look like a clown. Finally, a couple of months after he first told me he wanted a divorce, while I was still hoping to hold on to him, Tom just moved out.

More than anything else I remember feeling terror when he left. What would I do? My whole life, since I was sixteen years old, had been spent catering to, adoring, and helping Tom. By myself I was nothing and nobody. His total rejection of me underlined my already strong feeling of inadequacy. I had no job, no way to live, and nothing to live for.

After a couple of months my family glued me back together enough so that I was able to get a job as a receptionist in a doctor's office, the only kind of work I had ever done. I lived in constant pain, only half realizing where I was at times. I couldn't force myself to eat. I continued to lose weight and lived mostly on Hershey Bars and apples because I didn't have to cook them. When I finally became ravenous with hunger, I would just pick up a piece of candy or an apple and take a bite.

That was how I lived for nearly a year. I saw no one except people at work and my family. I lived in a one room apartment which I made no effort to keep clean. I crept home at night, lay down, and escaped into sleep. I didn't even turn on the television. I was barely alive.

One day my sister, Loretta, asked me to go with her to a painting class. It didn't require a lot of talent. It was just decorative painting—putting roses on trays, that sort of thing. At first I said I couldn't possibly go, but she went out and bought me some paints, came and picked me up, took me to the class, and enrolled me.

The first night I felt so awkward and inept that I was determined not to go back, but once again Loretta came to my apartment and picked me up. Gradually, I began to get mildly interested and my painting skill improved slightly.

As I neared the completion of my first project, a tray, I began thinking about what I should paint next. I decided on a wastebasket but I had a hard time deciding what colors to make it. The day came when I finally had to make up my mind because I was going to start my new project that evening. All day at work I thought about it. Should I make dark blue roses on a light blue background? Or maybe I should paint the whole thing in shades of beige. Throughout the entire day I imagined first one color scheme and then another.

As I left the office after work it occurred to me that for one whole day I had had relief from the pain of Tom's leaving me. "How could that happen?" I asked myself as I rode down in the elevator. I finally figured out that it was because I had spent the entire day thinking about what to do with my wastebasket. I had thought about something pleasant instead of something unpleasant, and I had been less miserable.

I'm sure it must seem ridiculous to many people that that was such a remarkable revelation to me. It is something millions of people already knew, and lots of books had been written on the subject of positive thinking. However, at that time it was a brand new idea to me that you felt happier when you thought about interesting, pleasant things than you did when you thought about painful things. Wonderful! That would be my key to survival.

The next day I woke up thinking about Tom again, but I didn't want the pain so on my way to work I began to search frantically for something pleasant to think about. The wastebasket problem was solved. What else could I think about? At last I decided what I would paint when I finished the wastebasket. That filled two more days of thinking. My painting projects were the only pleasant things I could think of to put in my mind so for the next two or three weeks I forced myself to think about them and allowed nothing else to enter my mind. I planned more projects than I could possibly paint before the classes ended in May.

I began hurting less and less. I was still lonely, of course, often blue and discouraged, but I kept my mind firmly on my painting. I had made what was, I am sure, the most valuable discovery I shall ever make in my entire life. I had learned that we can choose our thoughts and by choosing our thoughts we can, to a large extent, control whether we are happy or unhappy.

I felt a sense of panic when the art classes ended, though. What would I think about now? Again, Loretta came to my rescue. She suggested that I enroll in a course at the local community college. I decided on a literature course because I thought it would force me to do a lot of interesting reading, which would occupy my mind.

To my amazement, I discovered that I actually had a pretty fair brain. It had never really occurred to me that I could ever be anything but a receptionist in a doctor's office, but two teachers at the college encouraged me to keep taking courses, which I did. By my third semester I was carrying a full-time course load and working only part-time. Last year I graduated with a degree in English and this year I am teaching freshman English in a high school. Imagine me, the mousy little shadow of Tom, in charge of thirty teenagers, but I think I am doing well, and I love my job. This summer I will begin working toward my master's degree.

My almost primitive effort to keep happy thoughts instead of painful thoughts in my head led to another great turning point in my life. It caused me to literally stumble into college, which led to my having a career instead of just a job.

Now that I am no longer an ignoramus, I can occasionally quote something from literature which is appropriate for the occasion. I guess I'll show off my education by ending this story of my discovery about happy thinking with a quote from Plato. He said, "Our eyes can be turned toward the light as well as toward the dark . . . we all have eyes, though we do not know where to look."

Another young woman wrote about a turning point in her thinking which came about as a result of living in a commune in the 1960s. It is an excellent example of a turning point which was so subtle that a less perceptive person might not have recognized it as a turning point at all. Yet this young woman obviously considers it a milestone in her life, and it will give her readers insight into her character. Here is her story:

In 1968, to a middle class St. Louis girl, the world "commune" related only to Soviet public housing. I had no idea that in my own country drug-crazed and alienated flower children were beginning to set up communes in San Francisco's Haight Ashbury district. How could I possibly have imagined that I would, unwittingly, be instrumental in setting up what was probably the first commune in St. Louis?

My natural naiveté was accompanied by a rigid religious upbringing. A parochial education was supplemented by careful parental vigilance over boyfriends, movies, and moral fiber. The rigid Catholic Legion of Decency "A–2" movie rating ruled my social life. Forbidden films were evaluated solely on the basis of questionable language, excessive exposure of skin, or sexual overtones.

At nineteen, after a year of hassle-free dormitory life, I was determined to establish total independence. My friend, Sally, and I were unsuccessful in finding an apartment that fit both our fantasies and our limited resources. Finally, in August, we read a dream ad in the newspaper. "Beautiful old mansion—reasonably priced." Even the stars in our eyes could not blur the fact that "reasonably priced" bore no resemblance to our combined rent resources of $70 a month.

Determined to set up a household, I began looking at various options. We would simply have to acquire more roommates. I contacted two additional female friends and sold them on the concept of gracious living. I convinced Susan and Paulette that they should give up their snug little accommodations near work and school. The revelation that our "mansion" was a rambling old house in a declining neighborhood merely added a little romance to our adventure.

However, romance was not what I had in mind when I discovered, on moving day, that three men had somehow been absorbed into our household. Susan explained that Bob, Roger, and Richard were students needing low-cost housing. Besides, she consoled me, we will all feel safer with males around. My objections were unanimously overruled and my grudging consent to the men staying was the result of my determination to stay in the house.

Living with men! What would my parents say? Of course, they never said anything because they were never to know. On the few occasions when my parents visited, we hid all signs of masculine presence and treated the guys like dinner guests.

In the beginning, things in our house were very loose. We were the rage of the university and young business crowd. Everyone came to our house to party because we were considered free and "with it." At first I enjoyed the excitement and attention but after several weeks of feeding strangers, washing their dishes, and being force-fed their personal philosophies, I began to resent their intrusion into my life. I would come home between school and work to sleep because I had been up so late the previous night.

Most of my housemates soon quit school because it became impossible to study in the constant social ambiance of our home. Only Roger and I maintained our student status, but we were daily influenced by the bombardment of stimuli outside an academic setting.

I soon learned that life was not what I had assumed it to be. The people around me neither accepted the rigid moral commandments of my religious training nor the more pliant middle class Christian ethic which I prided myself on having recently absorbed. My values were constantly assaulted both by my housemates and by the incredible array of people who passed through our door. And while I considered myself intellectually "hip," rejection of one's family, of one's government, and of the "system" were ideas to which I had never before been exposed. During a moment of high drama at a party, I watched a raw-mouthed radical burn the flag. I was not so appalled by this patriotic desecration as I was by the underlying violence of his act. I was equally disturbed when an old high school acquaintance labeled my roommate a whore for kissing a black man.

Gradually, however, I began to realize that the moral values I had been taught could not serve as the sole barometer of my judgments. The most shocking individuals were often extremely protective toward me. Once someone teased me unmercifully about my virginity, and the worldly Richard firmly escorted the offending gentleman to the door. As my vulnerability became more evident, my high-living housemates and friends began to support my right to choose my own life-style.

We were semi-strangers living together, each learning to accept the other's divergent paths. When Linda left late one night to join her boyfriend in some Godforsaken eastern town, we all emptied our pockets to ensure her a safe journey and kept vigil by the phone all night in case of emergency. Within the year, we would all go our separate ways. During the time we lived in the house I did not (as the saying goes) "find myself," but my life was enriched by sharing in others' visions. And I learned something that was valuable for a narrow, sheltered young girl to know. I learned that other people's choices need not be a threat to me.

The next turning point story is about a family turning point rather than a personal turning point for the writer. I'm sure you will agree that it would have been a shame for this fascinating story to be lost to ensuing generations of the family. Yet that almost happened. If the writer hadn't decided to write the story of her life even the central figure of the story might never have heard it.

Margret grew up in Casablanca where her father was the British consul. Her family always spoke English at home, but since French was the official language of the country she studied it in school and was soon completely bilingual.

During World War II, she worked for the Allied Department of Psychological Warfare in North Africa. There she met her husband, Maxim, who worked in the same office.

Maxim's parents were Russian refugees who had escaped from Russia during the revolution and settled in Egypt, where Maxim was born and grew up. Maxim's family spoke Russian at home, but Arabic was the language spoken in his Egyptian school so he was equally at home with both languages. While in school, he also became fluent in both French and English.

Margret and Maxim were married in 1940 while the war was still going on, and Peter was born in 1944. When the war ended, Maxim got a job with the American occupation forces in Germany as a liaison officer between the Americans and Russians. At the time, Germany was overflowing with both Germans and displaced eastern Europeans who needed jobs, so servants were inexpensive and easy to come by. Margret and Maxim set up their household with a Polish nurse for Peter and a German maid.

Margret wrote the following fascinating story about Peter:

We brought up our son, Peter, in the manner of upper-class and upper middle-class Europeans. By that I mean that his life was in the nursery rather than with the adults of the family but this certainly doesn't mean he was neglected. Although he spent most of his time in his nursery, took his meals there with his nurse, and so on, he received frequent visits from adult members of the household throughout the day.

I, for example, always spent a full hour playing with him every morning after he had his breakfast and another hour after lunch before he took his nap. Frequently, during nice weather, I took him for walks in the park, or on a trip to the zoo, or to some other place where he could enjoy himself. When Maxim came home from work he always went directly to the nursery and spent an hour or an hour and a half before dinner, and either Maxim or I would read to Peter after he got in bed at night. He had, in fact, almost continuous attention. His nurse's sole duty was to take care of him, his clothes, and the nursery. Our maid was also fond of Peter and dropped in once or twice a day to greet him. Maxim's mother came from Egypt to visit us for several weeks each year and she was in and out of the nursery constantly, spoiling and pampering Peter.

Although Peter seemed to be an exceptionally bright child in every way, he was very slow in learning to talk. By the time he was four he was still jabbering unintelligibly and we became very fearful that he was retarded in some way. We consulted one doctor after another but got no help. By the time he was five and a half we were getting desperate. We finally found a German psychiatrist, Dr. Longreuter, who was interested in speech problems. He interviewed both Maxim and me

extensively about Peter and all of his associates. Since we had
no other children and none of our relatives or friends had children Peter's age, his circle of friends really included only his
nurse, our maid, his grandmother, and Maxim and me.

Dr. Longreuter had seen Peter for an hour twice a week for
eight or ten weeks when he called me to join him and Peter in
his office.

"Mrs. Sokoloff, what language do you speak when you talk
to Peter?"

"Why, French," I answered. "I am English, but I grew up in a
French-speaking country and consider it my native language."

"And you told me that your nurse is Polish, your maid is German, and your husband's mother is Russian. These people all
see Peter singly. Correct?"

I said that was usually the case.

"And do you think it would be fair to assume that each of
these women speaks to Peter in her native language? Wouldn't
that be the natural way to speak to a child?"

"Probably so." I answered. "I know for sure that Maxim speaks
to him in Arabic." I could see what Dr. Longreuter was getting
at. We were confusing Peter with too many languages, but if
that were the case why hadn't he picked up a few words from
each language instead of his meaningless jabbering?

"Mrs. Sokoloff," said the doctor, "don't you see what has
happened? Peter thinks each person has a language of his own.
What you call his jabbering is his language that he has made up
for himself because that is what he thought he was supposed to
do. He actually has a rather extensive vocabulary for a child his
age. It's just that you don't understand his words. I have been
cataloguing his sounds for weeks, and he always makes the same
sounds for the blocks that we play with, for the candy I give
him, and so forth. There's no doubt about it. He has made up
his own language. He has even worked out a sort of crude grammar. It is really quite a remarkable feat that he has performed."

You can imagine my relief and happiness. Discovering that Peter was not retarded was undoubtedly the happiest turning point in our family's life.

Since we were planning to immigrate to the United States when Maxim's job with the American occupation ended, we immediately began systematically to teach Peter English.

As we were working with him we watched for his little made-up words which the doctor had pointed out to us. Some of the words are still sort of pet words in our family. For example, Maxim and I always call a chair a "cote" and I frequently call Maxim "dupe," which was evidently Peter's word for father. Most of his words, though, were lost within a few weeks as he began to learn English, because he almost immediately forgot his own language. We were thrilled with his progress in English, but I couldn't help feeling a bit sad that his little language which he worked so hard to make up was being lost forever.

The woman who wrote this story told me that her husband was appointed to a position of simultaneous translator at the United Nations in New York only a few months after they began teaching Peter English. This made it possible for them to immigrate much sooner than they had expected.

"We were just engulfed by events for the next year," she said, "immigrating, getting settled in a new country, making new friends, getting Peter into school. And Maxim's new job was terribly demanding. We were so busy and our lives were moving so rapidly that Peter's language story got lost.

"Peter, of course, hadn't realized what was going on at the time. He just learned English as if it were a new game and that was that to him. Then as the years passed and two more children came along the fact that Peter had once made up his own language was practically forgotten. It never occurred to us to tell him about it when he was old enough to understand. I gave him this story to read after I wrote it for the turning points assignment, and he was absolutely fascinated by it. He is thirty years old now."

This is a wonderful example of how in the rush of our daily lives we fail to tell children facts which they would cherish about their heritage, even about their own lives.

In thinking about turning points remember that, as with the Sokoloffs, there can be family turning points as well as personal turning points. Remember, too, you may have had some turning points which were as subtle as those of the young girl whose thinking changed because she lived in a commune. These subtle turning points can be important to your story.

SIXTEEN

Children and the Things They Say

Anyone who has ever been around children for any length of time knows countless stories about bright, cute, funny, or touching things children say. Recalling these stories can have a double purpose. First, of course, if you write them down you are saving them for the children to read when they grow up and you are also saving them for future generations.

A second reason for preserving these stories is that telling them is a wonderful way to get the children and young people in your family interested in family history. Sometimes young people are in such a hurry that they think primarily of the present, very little of the future, and almost never of the past. However, I must tell you something that happened at my breakfast table one Saturday morning. My niece and nephew and their three children, who ranged in age from twelve to seventeen, were visiting me from out of town. The children had been allowed to come to the table in their bathing suits because one of the big things they were looking forward to during the visit was swimming in the pool at my condominium. They wanted to be all ready to hop into the pool the minute they finished eating.

For some reason we adults began remembering cute things the kids had said and done when they were little—things they didn't remember. Each story we told reminded us of another and the children laughed uproariously at themselves and at each other as they listened and begged for more. Then, to our surprise, they began asking about the childhood of the adults and we all three began telling stories about when we were little. We gradually began remembering stories from our later lives and told them, too.

The children loved all of our stories—loved them so much, in fact, that they never made it into the pool. A couple of hours passed while we continued to sit at the table and talk. Finally someone looked at the clock and discovered it was time for all of us to dress for an appointment. What a wonderful family visit we had! And it all started with our telling the kids about themselves.

I have shared this story with people in my classes who have wondered how they could get children interested in their family heritage. Several have reported that they tried it and that it worked. They started telling the kids about themselves and the kids discovered that family history isn't a dull abstraction. It's about real people—themselves, their parents, and other people they know. One woman told the class that after she started telling her grandchildren about themselves they began asking her to read to them from "the history book you're writing, grandma."

Most stories about the things children say aren't very complicated and you probably don't need any samples to help you write them, but here are a couple I thought you might enjoy. The first one is certainly a wonderful example of sharing wisdom with your readers.

It happened many years ago, but it could have happened yesterday. The memory is so vivid.

One evening at the dinner table my wife, Rose, and I were engaged in a discussion. We had been having a lot of them lately.

We thought it was a discussion until our five-year-old son, John, blurted out, "Why don't we fight on Tuesdays only?"

Joy, his sister, who was two years older, echoed the plea, "Yes, can't we please?"

John, bold and impetuous, was looking down at his plate. He was almost angry. Joy, quiet and gentle, was near tears.

To John, Tuesday was just a figure of speech. He was telling us in his own way to stop arguing and save it for another day. Simple and direct, like a child, it couldn't have been more effective.

Rose and I were silent. We looked at our children, we looked at each other, and we looked at ourselves. What we saw made us unhappy and ashamed. We had fallen into the very bad habit of taking out our frustrations on each other at the worst possible time and place—at the dinner table before our children. We had ignored the fact that children, though little, are sensitive people, as capable of feelings as any grown up, maybe even more so.

After a few moments I said, "Sure, let's table this until Tuesday."

"Table it 'til Tuesday" became a catch phrase with magic power. We used it often and we still use it. It helped change our lives for the better.

We soon learned that many of the seemingly insurmountable problems were nothing of the sort. We discovered that it was just as easy to make mole hills out of mountains as vice-versa. By the time "Tuesday" came around, the problem had often disappeared or had become so trivial that it was easily disposed of. Sometimes we even forgot what the problem was.

Joy and John are out on their own now. Rose and I are alone. We think of the past often and have many happy memories but the one that gives us the greatest pleasure is living again that evening long ago when our children gave us a lifetime gift by teaching us to "table it until Tuesday."

This next story typifies many of the hilarious things children say and do as they try to find their way around in the world. It was written by a grandmother about her four-year-old granddaughter, whose mother had been trying to teach her about the concept of privacy. The little girl had been told repeatedly that when she came to a closed door she must always knock or call before opening it because the person on the other side of the door might want some privacy.

One day when I was sitting in the bathtub I heard Shona's little voice calling, "Grandmother, do you want some privacy?"

I called back, "Yes, dear, I would like some privacy for a few minutes." The words were just out of my mouth when the door opened and Shona popped into the room.

"Okay," she said as she closed the door behind her, "I'll shut the door so you can have some privacy while I watch you take your bath."

A cartoon called "Family Circus," which appears in my newspaper and probably in yours, is based almost entirely on this kind of innocent humor—little kids who are doing their best to get along on the planet on which they arrived so recently. If it's in your newspaper and if you haven't been reading it, by all means start. It's bound to remind you of many wonderful things you have heard children say.

SEVENTEEN

Inventions

I believe the assignment on inventions has revealed to me greater differences between my students who are sixty and over and my students who are thirty-five and under than any other assignment. The older students are able to think of so many inventions which appeared during their lifetime that there is barely room to list all of them on their memory bank Invention page: the first automobile, the first motion picture, the first talking picture, the first radio, the first electric light, the first telephone, the first permanent wave machine, the first electric refrigerator, and on and on. We have a lot of laughs in class about the student's first experiences with various inventions, and I get the feeling that to this day they have a sense of wonder that it all happened. It is as if they are still able to recapture that first feeling of near-disbelief that someone had done something so outlandish as to invent a horseless carriage.

On the other hand, my younger students, who have been surrounded by an explosion of technology all of their lives, have trouble coming up with inventions about which to write. When I asked my first class of young students to mention some inventions they remembered there was a rather bemused silence. Finally, a thirty-one-year-old woman remarked rather sheepishly, "I'm sure there have been lots of things, but it seems like everything has just always been here." Then she brightened as if pleased to be able to help and said, "I know something—microwave ovens!"

Another student, whose furrowed brow indicated that he had been doing some hard thinking, added, "This isn't exactly an invention, but I remember when we didn't have fast foods. I mean, you could always get a hamburger but you had to wait for them to make it, and you couldn't get fried fish and fried chicken and Mexican food just by walking up to a counter or driving past a window."

Finally, someone mentioned what I had expected all of them to think of immediately. "Well," he said, "there's space travel—going to the moon." This young man's statement was followed by a class discussion which absolutely amazed me. The students conceded that the moon shot certainly had been interesting and they acknowledged that they should have thought of it without any hesitation when I first asked about inventions. However, they also generally agreed that they hadn't really been astounded by it. I expressed surprise at their casual attitude and asked how they accounted for it.

One student explained in a very matter-of-fact way. "Well, I guess we knew it was just a matter of time until someone would do it. I think we all understood pretty well how it would work from reading science fiction."

I realized that he was right. Science fiction is one of the most popular forms of literature among today's young people, and good science fiction is based on sound scientific principles. Consequently, it is frequently a foreshadowing of things to come. Also, an entire academic discipline has grown up around futurism. Not infrequently a futurist from some university appears on television telling us what kind of technical and social developments we can expect in the next few years.

Even the cartoons children watch condition them to expect ever-greater technological developments. Sam, a little six-year-old friend of mine, brought this fact about cartoons home to me one day when his mother was in the midst of an unusually heavy burden of house-work. Sam, seeing his mother somewhat overwhelmed by her tasks, asked in an effort to be helpful, "Mommy, when can we get a robot?" His mother explained that the day before he had seen a cartoon on television in which the mother, before leaving for her office, had programmed the family robot for the day's housekeeping duties. Little wonder that children are no longer astounded by new technology. They just wonder why it wasn't available sooner.

I can't help feeling a little sad about all of this. I am certainly not one who longs for "the good old days." I would hate to give up my dishwasher, my plane trips, my automatic washer, and so on. What I can't help regretting, though, is the fact that today's children and young people have, to a very great extent, missed the opportunity to enjoy a sense of wonder and surprise. Even my generation, which has always had cars, airplanes, electric refrigerators, and movies, has experienced a few thrills of discovery. I remember how excited I was when I saw television for the first time, and I was absolutely flabbergasted by aluminum foil.

Working with my younger students has caused me to realize all over again how vitally important it is for older people to write about their lives and times. We need to help today's (and tomorrow's) children and young people experience, if only vicariously, the innocence and wonder that has been denied their generations. They can look at pictures of horses and buggies, but that isn't enough. They can read about the invention of the automobile, but that isn't enough. They need an opportunity to know how it felt for their own ancestors to ride in a horse-drawn buggy and how it felt for them to see an automobile for the first time.

If you belong to a generation that had the privilege of being astounded by each new invention that came along, try to recapture in as much detail as possible the excitement of discovery so you can share it with your readers. I think you will agree that the seventy-five-year-old woman who wrote the story below was able to do that:

Very vivid in my memory is the first time I tasted ice cream. I was about six and my two sisters were seven and two. We were living in Lamoni, Iowa, at the time. I think it must have been about 1911.

There had been a hard rain in the late afternoon and early evening, and as the rain almost stopped the sun came out. Mama and we girls were out in the yard looking at a beautiful rainbow, a wonderful sight to us. Then we saw papa coming through the orchard east of our house, and in his hand was a little cardboard bucket with a wire handle. We had no idea what was in the little bucket, but mama said it was papa's surprise for us. And what a surprise—ice cream! Mama quickly divided it into dishes and we all had a feast. I never see a rainbow to this day without thinking of that momentous occasion.

Later, after there was an ice house in Lamoni, we had an ice cream freezer at home, and with cream from our Jersey cow, mama made wonderful custard, and papa turned the crank on the freezer. Often it had fresh strawberries from our own garden in it. Delicious!

By the time this woman wrote her story she had eaten her share of Howard Johnson's and Baskin and Robbins's dozens of flavors of ice cream. Yet she remembers so vividly and described so graphically her first bite of ice cream that she almost made us taste it, too. She also managed to give us a delightful glimpse of a close and loving family in an innocent time when an evening around an ice cream freezer was a joyful event. I think it is important for young people to have an opportunity to see this picture.

When you are writing about your first encounter with new inventions, set the stage for the story of your great discovery just as the woman did who wrote about the ice cream and as one of the my students did when he wrote the following story. He wrote it in 1921, when he was sixteen and living on a farm near a small Kansas town. He and his father, as was their custom, went into town on a Saturday night:

I was getting very tired and all of the friends I had been with had gone home so I set out in search of my father. I went to all of his usual haunts, the Odd Fellows Hall, and so on, but I couldn't find him. I decided he must be at a lodge where I knew he sometimes enjoyed being in a card game. When I entered the lodge hall I found my dear dad and many other important men of the town in the process of taking off long white robes and pointed white hoods which covered their faces.

Needless to say, my arrival caused great consternation among the men because the Ku Klux Klan was supposed to be a secret society. Here was this youth who had seen some of the most prominent men of the town disrobing—this was serious!

They called the Grand Dragon of Kansas in Topeka and told him of the situation. He said there was no way out except that I must be made to join the Klan so that I would be constrained from talking about it by the oath of secrecy that I would have to take. I was under age for membership but he authorized my joining. And that is how on the same night I became the youngest member of the Ku Klux Klan and discovered that one could call on the telephone between two cities which were nearly a hundred miles apart.

I hasten to add that this man was one of the most genuinely humane people I have ever met and the last person who would have deliberately joined the Ku Klux Klan. He ends his story by saying that at first the robes, the hoods, the cross burning were heady stuff to a teenager. However, he soon became disenchanted with the Klan because young as he was, he could not accept its teachings, noting that "it would be hard to find more virulent trash than the teachings to which we were subjected."

I have concluded that the best way for young people to use the assignment on inventions is as a basis for questioning their parents, grandparents, and great grandparents. If you are one of my younger readers, I urge you to ask older persons about their memories of inventions. You may be surprised at the stories you will hear. For example, the woman who wrote about tasting ice cream for the first time has an eleven-year-old granddaughter who could scarcely believe that there was ever a time when her grandmother had never heard of ice cream.

EIGHTEEN

Holidays

Of course, having taught this course to many students, I have an almost endless supply of holiday stories. It was difficult to know which ones to select for this book. Most, but not all, of the stories centered around family. Significantly, some of the happiest holiday memories seem to be those which didn't involve large expenditures of money. One particularly nice story was written by a woman who was a child during the depression:

We didn't get a single new present that year. There just wasn't any money, but my mother gathered up scraps of material and must have worked for weeks making a nice wardrobe for the doll I had received the year before when times were better. I'm sure she didn't buy anything new except maybe a little bit of trimming, because I recognized every piece of cloth as being left from some piece of family clothing.

My father, who I knew hated doing any kind of carpentry or fix-it type work, asked a friend to show him how to make doll furniture. Out of little scraps of wood—mostly free orange crates from the grocery store, I think—he made a little table and four chairs and a wardrobe for my doll.

I remember that as a happy Christmas. I was only about five or six but I sensed that times were hard and that my parents had poured a lot of love into those gifts.

The next holiday story I selected is about a little bit of Americana which has all but disappeared—the one room school house. It sounds like a story from long ago, right out of *The Little House on the Prairie*, yet the woman who wrote it is only in her late fifties. This story reminds us all over again of how young our country is, how rapidly times are changing, and how important it is to write down everything we can think of to help preserve our heritage.

When I was in the sixth grade my family moved from the city to the country. I thought my life was over and that nothing could be as awful as living on a farm with outside plumbing and going to a one room school.

Sometimes things were rough for me at school. Some of the children were nice to me but many resented me and never let me forget that I was "the city kid." To be absolutely honest I expect part of their attitude stemmed from the fact that I, too, made a point of the fact that I was "the city kid."

In spite of the fact that I used to go home from school and cry my eyes out because I was so lonely and missed my friends from town, and in spite of the fact that I always hated the farm, I remember those three years as some of the happiest school days of my life because of the school's only teacher, Miss Chiles.

There were twelve students and eight grades. Can you imagine all the different classes she had to teach? It seems impossible that she could manage, but she did, and do you know something? We all learned to read, write, spell, do arithmetic, understand history and geography, and appreciate paintings, books, and music. We didn't have any special visual aids, cassettes, piped in educational television, or any of the many educational tools that schools have today. We just had one very dedicated teacher.

In addition to teaching her many classes, Miss Chiles planned wonderful holiday parties for us. On Halloween we brought costumes from home, and Miss Chiles arranged with various farmers' wives who lived near the school to let us change into our costumes at their houses.

Soon after lunch on the day of the party Miss Chiles made us all put our heads down on our desks and close our eyes. Then she tiptoed quietly around and dismissed first one and then another, telling us where we were supposed to go to change. As soon as one student was out of sight of the school she dismissed the next one. That way we wouldn't know who was dressing where, so we didn't know who was behind each mask when we came walking back to the school for the party at two o'clock. We all tried to guess who was who, which really wasn't very hard since there were so few children of such obviously assorted sizes. We made a big thing of guessing, though.

While we were gone to get into our costumes Miss Chiles got food and decorations out of her car. Sometimes her mother came to help her. They acted as if they thought throwing a kid party was the most fun a person could have.

Easter was another special holiday. Miss Chiles hid dozens of colored Easter eggs all over the yard—or inside if the weather was bad. There were big chocolate rabbits for prizes for the one who found the most eggs, and an Easter basket full of candy bars for the one who won pin-the-tail-on-the-rabbit. There were prizes for everything. If there wasn't a legitimate reason for you to get a prize, Miss Chiles made one up. It was impossible not to win a prize at one of Miss Chiles's Easter parties.

Christmas was an evening party with all of the mothers bringing wonderful homemade cakes, pies, and cookies. We made decorations for the school and presented a play on which we had been working for weeks. Somehow Miss Chiles arranged for every child, no matter how old or how young, how bright or how dull, to have a part in the play. The Christmas party was a major event, not just for us children, but for the whole community.

Then, of course, there were Valentine boxes, St. Patrick's Day celebrations, even April Fool jokes. Miss Chiles never missed a chance to have a party. When a new student came to the school she called his mother and asked what kind of cake was his favorite. Then on that child's birthday that was the kind of cake Miss Chiles baked. During the last week of school we had one big birthday party for everyone who had a birthday during the summer.

I want to call your attention to a little bit of honesty in this story. I imagine that the woman who wrote it hated the children who made fun of her for being from the city. However, in retrospect she admits that a lot of their meanness was probably her own fault. She could have remained self-righteous about the children's cruelty or she could have left out the conflict entirely and made her story just an idyllic picture of life in a country school. Instead, she included all of her unhappiness, which made it seem real, and which will help her readers understand some of the struggles she had as a city child moving to a farm. Thus, although this is a holiday story and a one room schoolhouse story, it is more than that. It is the writer's personal story too. Remember ground rule number three—Be honest, and ground rule number four—Don't let your story be just a sterile recital of events.

Many students have written about a Christmas that stands out in their memory because they or someone they knew did something especially nice for another person. Here's a story one man wrote about one such Christmas:

My father had an incomparable Christmas spirit. On Christmas Eve he always left a thermos of hot coffee and a plate of cookies on a little table by the fireplace so Santa could have a snack after leaving our gifts under the tree. My sister Melissa and I, impressionable pre-schoolers, were delighted when we saw the obviously used coffee cup and cookie crumbs the following morning.

One Christmas morning when Melissa and I hurried to see if Santa had consumed his snack, Melissa noted with a shout that there was a present in the fireplace.

"Well, I'll be darned!" my dad exclaimed as he brushed the soot off the package. "Santa must have dropped this out of his bag by mistake when he started back up the chimney." Dad looked at the tag on the brightly wrapped package and said, "Why, this is Wayne's package; he must have been next on Santa's list." Wayne was a playmate of ours who lived a few houses down the street. Dad said, "We'll have to take it to Wayne and explain what happened."

Wayne's parents were poor and Dad said the gift would mean a lot to him. We would go to Wayne's house right after we opened our gifts.

We took the package to Wayne and explained Santa's mistake. The look of joy on Wayne's face as he opened the gift, a nice book, convinced us that Dad was right. There hadn't been many presents under the tree at Wayne's house.

After I married and my wife and I had children of our own, my dad continued to make our holiday season very special. His Christmas spirit never waned.

After his passing I always tried to make Christmas at our house a notable day, one that might linger in our children's memory like that one Christmas remains in mine.*

Can you remember a holiday when you or someone you know did something especially thoughtful for someone else? One of my students wrote about the time she and her family gave away their Christmas tree. And do you remember the Christmas story in Louisa Mae Alcott's *Little Women* when the March family gave away their Christmas dinner?

When I first gave the holiday assignment I was expecting a lot of happy stories about memories of wonderful holidays, and I have heard many of those. However, I have also heard many unhappy holiday stories.

The following holiday story was written by a young Polish woman who married an American and came to this country with him:

It happened one year ago. My first Christmas in Chicago is kept in my mind as the worst day of my life.

I was sitting among my husband's family with great sadness in my soul. I haven't liked them and they haven't liked me. Our Christmas wishes were insincere. "Why must I do this?" I asked myself. "Only for my husband, only for my love," I answered. I couldn't cry among them because they never could understand me. They couldn't imagine that my family Christmas in Poland had been so different.

Oh how wonderful had been Christmas time at my home! Everybody was happy, merry, and sincere in their wishes. We were forever singing Christmas carols during breaks between the meals. These are the unforgettable moments, which are always fresh in my memory.

But the present time was so different that it was not possible to feel any family spirit. My husband was very gentle to me and understood my loneliness, but he couldn't change anything. I was thinking about my mother and our love, and only these thoughts helped me to survive this time. These thoughts have always brightened my sadness.

I very often had to hide in the bathroom, when I could cry without witnesses! I was crying like a lost child, like a lonely bird without a nest. I was crying for help. But who could help me? "Only I can help myself," repeated my thoughts, which went round and round incessantly.

People are very different with different personalities, and if we don't make efforts to understand them, it is impossible for us to live together. Only common sense could help me to adopt the new family and to accept their habits.

To balance this story this young woman must, of course, write a description of Christmas in Poland, which will give her children and their children a sense of their Polish heritage. However, her story would be incomplete without this bleak story of her first American Christmas.

Another lonely holiday story was written by a retired minister. He wrote about arriving in Los Angeles on the day before Thanksgiving to take his first job as an assistant pastor in a large church:

I didn't actually have to report to work until the Monday after Thanksgiving, but I didn't have either time or money to go home to West Virginia after leaving the seminary just before Thanksgiving, so I went straight to Los Angeles.

I'm sure many members of the congregation as well as the minister and his wife would have invited me for Thanksgiving dinner if they had known I was alone, but I was too shy to let them know. I just had Thanksgiving dinner at a corner drug store. It was a terrible day because our family always made a lot out of holidays.

Have you heard the saying that the teacher learns from the student? That certainly happened in my case when I read about some of my students' lonely holidays.

As it happens, for forty years I have had marvelous Christmases. I always spend the holiday with my nephew and his family, my niece and her family, my sister and, before she died, my mother.

The nature of our jobs has made it possible for us to spend from three days to a week away from work so our celebrations are non-stop for several days. Sometimes we have all been living in different states, but we have always managed to gather at either my nephew's or my sister's house.

We all, including the children, love to cook. There are several dishes which we have traditionally every year, but throughout the year we all keep an eye out for special new recipes we want to share at Christmas. We arrive not only with our Christmas presents but also with our recipes, our ingredients, and sometimes even our own cooking utensils. We are as great hams about our cooking as actors are about their acting. I guess you could say we really "show off" for each other. It's great eating and great fun. It's three to five days of visiting, church going, present giving, cooking, eating, game playing, and it's one of the high points of my year.

Naturally, when it came time to write about holidays I wrote about these wonderful Christmases, which I hope will continue for years to come. But let me tell you I have had some dreary and lonely Christmases, too. A couple were positively awful. Their memory had been all but blotted out by recent happy Christmases until some of my students' lonely holiday stories brought them back to me. I intend now to write about how I survived them and put the stories in my book.

Maybe someone, who-knows-how-many generations hence, will be feeling a little down and will read what I have written and say, "Well, look how bad things were for her and then see how much better they got."

The possibility of future generations being affected by what we write came home to me forcefully when I was editing the *Overland Journal*. A writer submitted an article that included many stories written by people describing how they celebrated the Fourth of July on the Oregon Trail. I was amazed by the amount of mail I received from readers thanking me for the article. Several of them said they had read it at family Fourth of July celebrations. One woman wrote, "There were tears in a lot of eyes when I stopped reading." Another writer said, "It made me wonder when I stopped thinking of the Fourth as Independence Day and started thinking of it as just another day off from work to go fishing."

I thought you might like to read a few of these stories written so long ago. There's a poignancy in some of them because the writers knew that when they crossed the Missouri River they were leaving the United States, probably forever. As one diarist wrote, "We were expatriating ourselves, but we didn't feel any less patriotic about our country. Maybe we felt even more patriotic than we did at home."

Most of the trains left sometime in early May. They couldn't leave earlier because the grass was not tall enough to provide adequate food for the oxen pulling the wagons, but they couldn't leave much later than the middle of May because they would run into snow in the Blue Mountains of Oregon. This meant that by the Fourth of July most of the trains were somewhere in central Wyoming and hadn't yet encountered the terrible hardships of deserts, mountains, dwindling supplies, and exhausted oxen and still had energy and inclination to celebrate.

Some travelers prepared for the Independence Day celebration before they left home. Others, like people in the following story improvised:

Some young ladies were seated on the grass talking over the problem of manufacturing Old Glory to wave over our festivities. The question was where to obtain material to make it. One lady brought out a sheet, and another contributed a skirt for the red stripes. Another lady ran to her tent and brought forth a blue jacket saying, "Here, take this; it will do for the field." After the celebration was over we drew lots to see who would get to keep this wonderful flag.

An Englishman wrote:

Six of us Britishers were traveling in a Yankee company. Some of the Yanks came to us and said they wanted to celebrate American independence on the Fourth of July if it wouldn't offend us. We said we had no objection, so as midnight on the Third came around there was a peppery salvo of revolvers and rifles. They concocted a bucket of capital punch, and we were all so desirous of delivering complimentary toasts about each other's country that our wives finally told us we had better go to bed and sleep off our patriotism so we could get a good start on our journey the next morning.

Another diarist described a somewhat more formal celebration:

Today is the seventy-fourth anniversary of our glorious independence. We pitched one of the tents a short distance from the camp and placed seats in it for the orators. At twelve o'clock we formed a procession and marched to the tent singing "The Star Spangled Banner."

We all sat on the ground and listened to a prayer by Mr. Hobart, then remarks and the reading of the Declaration of Independence by Mr. Pratt, and an address by Mr. Sexton. Then Mr. Lambert played "Hail Columbia" on his fiddle. We then had a fine meal consisting of roast antelope, roast sage hen, roast rabbit, antelope stew, sage hen stew, rabbit stew, antelope potpie, fried sage hen, Irish potatoes (brought from Illinois), rice, Boston baked beans, fresh baked bread, jelly cake, sweet mountain water cake, and a fruit cake which a lady had brought all the way from Missouri for the celebration. She had packed it in a tight tin container filled with whiskey to keep it moist and give it flavor. All of the other food, of course, was cooked over an open fire. It took many of the ladies of our company only a week or so on the trail to learn to cook and bake very well over a camp fire.

There are quite a number of stories about travelers, particularly children, wandering away from camp and getting lost. Some of the stories ended happily but some did not. This story happens to have a happy ending:

We were getting quite worried about three young ladies who had disappeared. We were afraid they might have wandered off and gotten lost. Just as we were ready to organize a search party they emerged from behind a huge boulder looking very pleased with themselves. They had taken the company's flag with them and cut out a star for Oregon and sewed it on the field. We gave them high praise and left the new star in place. (It would be eleven years before Oregon would become a state and get its own star on an official flag.)

NINETEEN

Politics

When we come to the assignment on politics many of my students say, "Well, I won't have anything to say about that. I've never been mixed up in politics." We then have a discussion about the fact that politics doesn't necessarily mean party politics. How government, its laws and institutions affect our lives can come under the heading of politics.

All women, whether they realize it or not, have been involved in politics since the day they were born because so many laws apply to them which don't apply to men. Many problems which women have had through the years have been caused by these laws. Blacks, too, are affected by politics even if they never enter a voting booth. The Civil Rights Movement was politics. If we pay taxes we are affected by politics. If we go to school we are affected by politics. In short, if we are alive we are affected by politics. The story of the politics of your day can be an important reflection of your times and thus an important part of your story.

Sometimes our very lack of conscious involvement in politics is the basis for a revealing story about ourselves. This was the case with a woman in her eighties who wrote the following story:

I wasn't active in the suffrage movement when I was young so it's no thanks to me that I have the vote today. I feel a little guilty sometimes that I didn't work in the movement because I always resented not being allowed to vote. I just couldn't bring myself to do anything about it, though, because I thought the things women had to do to win the vote—demonstrating, marching in the streets, holding rallies, and all that sort of thing—were not ladylike.

I got married in 1915 so I was a young bride when the last big push was on before we finally got the vote in 1919. One part of me wanted to be a proper, respectable housewife and the other part of me felt angry because I couldn't vote. I guess what happened is that the respectable housewife won out.

I might point out, I suppose as sort of an excuse for myself, that the women today who are working for the Equal Rights Amendment don't know how lucky they are to have support from a good many newspapers, magazines, and television, and even from a lot of men. There are even several magazines devoted entirely to the feminist movement. You know, back when the suffragettes were fighting to get the vote even most of the women's magazines didn't favor votes for women.

The only time I ever mentioned the suffrage movement to my husband was once when one of my favorite women's magazines wrote a scathing editorial against some suffragettes who demonstrated outside the White House.

It was during World War I. Wilson had just made his famous speech about fighting the war to "make the world safe for democracy." The suffragettes carried banners saying that America was not a democracy because not all of its citizens were allowed to vote. Some of the banners pointed out that we were way behind Russia because Russian women had equal rights with men.

The editorial said that Russian women through several generations had earned the right to vote by playing both men's and women's parts in the world, "as did our own pioneer grand-mothers." It went on to say that what America needed was not more votes but more love from its citizens and that by demanding the vote in time of war women were not showing that love. The editorial ended by expressing satisfaction that the demonstrating suffragettes had been dragged off to jail.

I was so mad when I read that that I thought I would explode. I was accustomed to reading this kind of tirade against suffragettes in the general press, and although I didn't read men's magazines I expected that they would express the same sentiment. I guess I thought this was to be expected, but to read such an editorial in a women's magazine made me furious. When my husband came home from work I just blew up.

I said, "I want you to read this awful thing. What do they mean American women haven't won the right to vote? What did men do to win the right to vote? And what good did it do our pioneer grandmothers to do both men's and women's work? They didn't get the vote. As soon as men could afford to, they stuck us in hot houses like plants and wouldn't let us do both men's and women's work if we wanted to. Anyway, why should women be expected to do both men's and women's work in order to get the vote? Men aren't expected to do both. They are only expected to do men's work. It isn't fair!"

My poor husband looked very startled at my outburst. I couldn't tell whether there was hurt in his eyes or embarrassment or what, but there was certainly surprise. I was immediately sorry that I had exploded to my kind and gentle husband, and I kissed him, took his hat, and told him that dinner was nearly ready. We never mentioned votes for women again.

I wish I could say that I had been one of those brave women who did so much for all of us, but the fact is that I wasn't. Looking back now I think I was just a ninny.

The next story, which was written by a young black man in a community college in Chicago, is a civil rights story. It had nothing to do with party politics, but it is a political story nonetheless, and a tragic one:

On a hot summer afternoon in 1968, when I was nine years old, Dr. Martin Luther King was shot and killed. After the news had gotten on the streets that King was dead, both blacks and whites went wild and started acting with mass rage. Riots broke out all over the United States; people went crazy in cities, suburbs, and even in the country.

In Chicago, people shot and killed other people and started acting like a bunch of fools. Some were killed while trying to rob others and some were killed for just walking the streets.

The governor of the state called in the National Guard, and the guardsmen were told that anyone on the street was to be put in jail. I got the picture and ran home, but before I made it to my house, I saw a guard turn and fire a couple of rounds at people running down the street. After I saw that, I ran faster toward home.

When I got up to the door, I tried to open it but it was locked. I began to beat on the green wooden door and to cry because I was scared now. When the door finally opened, I saw my mother. She was on her knees and she quickly yanked me to the floor. After she pulled me down, she slammed the door and said to be quiet.

I could hear all kinds of guns going off with loud booms and bangs and they seemed to grow louder as the time went on, but my mother didn't worry, she just said quietly and kept saying, "It will be all right when your father gets home."

But this was not to be, because my father was shot in the head as he was coming home from work. It happened right outside our door.

We heard a very loud boom and then a scream. We heard moaning and groaning and then my mother's name. At first she thought the call was for someone else and she didn't move, but then she heard the voice again and it was calling her name. The next thing I knew, she was up on her feet and heading for the door. She flung it open as if it were a little toy and ran out onto the porch and disappeared around the corner. I heard a scream, but was too afraid to see what had happened. My little brother jumped up and ran out the door right behind me.

Then my mother started dragging my father into our house. At this time, a neighbor lady named Miss Jones started to scream. She had seen what was going on. Without another word, she too was on her knees pulling my father toward the door. When they pulled him inside we were told to get some towels. When I looked up, I could see my little brother; he was bleeding from the chest. My sister grabbed him and held a towel over the blood.

Next came getting towels for my father. I couldn't see where he was shot, but I knew it was bad because I could see all the blood.

Then Miss Jones ran out of the apartment to call an ambulance, but she came back and said they would not come into our neighborhood, so my mother got on the phone and called a couple of my relatives. They were there within minutes, and they rushed my father and brother to the hospital. My father was dead on arrival and my brother had a bullet wound in his chest. They got the bullet out of his chest, but kept him in the hospital for a while.

When I heard the news, I started to cry and so did everyone else in the house.

Later, after the news had spread and the shouting had died down, we received a letter from a man saying he was sorry about what had happened. He sent flowers to the funeral.

The more I think of what happened and how my father was taken away from me and almost my little brother too, it makes me feel so sad, and I just want to take a gun and kill the first white face I see, but that would only get me in trouble. I now have learned how to hide my feelings and not show my anger even though sometimes I feel like I could blow up the world.

Of course some of my students have been actively involved in politics. One woman in her late forties who was one of the founders of her local Women's Political Caucus wrote the following story:

I felt that I had been unfairly treated in business all of my life because of being a woman, so when some Kansas City women wanted to start a Women's Political Caucus I decided to help them. I knew I wanted to fight for women's rights, but I didn't exactly realize what that meant in terms of politics. I found out it meant getting people out to vote for candidates who favor women's issues.

In February someone was explaining to me what a political ward was and in August I was organizing one. Missouri is a caucus state, and delegates to the state convention are elected at local ward meetings. The group that gets the most people out to its ward meeting gets the largest representation at the state convention.

Another woman and I made speeches, spent hours on the telephone, and did everything we could think of to get people to come to the ward meeting to vote for delegates who would favor George McGovern. He was our candidate because he seemed to favor more women's issues than any other presidential candidate in either party.

The night of our ward meeting 325 people showed up to vote for McGovern delegates compared with only 25 regular Democrats, which is what all the Democrats who weren't for McGovern were called that year. On the news that night the television commentator said our ward had had the biggest sweep for McGovern of any ward in the city. He talked about the "stunning defeat" of the regular Democrats and about the fact that no one around the studio could remember ever having heard of such a turnout for a ward meeting.

What a heady night that was! I, a complete political novice, had in a small way made political history. Several other wards won big for McGovern that night, many of them because of the work of novices like me from the Women's Political Caucus. We thought all we had to do from then on was work hard and our cause of women's rights would be won.

We were sure that since we had demonstrated what great politicians we were all of the candidates would be courting us, trying desperately to get us on their side. We were in for a big surprise when we got to the state convention at Jefferson City.

We, like many other groups, set up a hospitality room in the motel where most of the candidates were staying, and we invited the governor and the chairman of the state Democratic committee to come and get acquainted. Governor Warren Hearnes completely ignored our invitation. The state chairman, whose name I don't remember, dropped in at about 1:00 a.m. He was roaring drunk and began hugging and pawing all of us and saying things like, "I don't know why you girls think I don't like the ladies. Why, I love the ladies!" Then he added to the president of the caucus, "But if you try to foul me up at the convention tomorrow, I'll stomp on your pretty little asses."

He was certainly a man of his word. He tramped all over us at the convention the next day. That year, for the first time, the Democratic party had set delegate quotas for minorities and women to the national convention. They were supposed to be represented in proportion to their percentage of the population. We naively thought Missouri politicians would abide by these rules.

Instead, they went right ahead electing practically all male delegates to the national convention. Several times during the convention women rose to remind the chairman of the quotas. After the first two women spoke the chairman silenced them by simply turning off every mike into which a woman started to speak.

As of this writing, December, 1979, both Governor Hearnes and that state chairman have disappeared from the political scene. However, women still aren't faring very well in Missouri, which so far has refused to ratify the Equal Rights Amendment.

Happily, things have changed since 1979. The woman who worked with my student to organize the ward and who was one of the women prevented from speaking at the state convention is now a U.S. Congresswoman.

TWENTY

Animals

I found the Animals assignment particularly interesting. When I originally thought of animals as a category for stories I was thinking of stories about family pets. Once again I had failed to realize how young our country is. Nearly all of the animal stories in my first class of older students were about wild animals. One woman wrote about the man who came through her small Missouri town every fall selling wild horses which he or someone else had captured in the West. "Broncos, we called them," she said, "and then a few weeks later a bronco buster who was working with the salesman would come through and break the horses for us. That's how most people got their horses in those days."

A young man wrote an animal story that had nothing to do with family pets. He was an ex-GI who had been stationed in Germany. He wrote about visiting the Berlin Zoo, which is one of the great zoos of the world.

Farm animals, too, were favorite topics. Here's one of my favorite farm animal stories:

It was back in 1896 in Norton County, Kansas, just before Thanksgiving. My parents climbed to the high spring seat on the lumber wagon to drive into Alema to arrange for the sale of their two dozen turkeys.

Before leaving Papa told my brother, Jessie, and me to carry several bushels of rotting apples from the cellar and put them in the yard so he could load them and cart them away.

Mama and Papa had barely driven out of sight when two neighbor boys arrived to spend the day with us. The four of us carried the dripping, mushy apples into the yard. A few weeks earlier I had spilled some seed corn among the apples when I reached over them to get the corn that was on the shelf in back of the apple bin.

The turkeys scrambled over the pile of apples in the yard, eating both the corn and the apples. We went to play.

When we came back several turkeys were sprawled out on the ground. Others were staggering and reeling and about to topple over. I was terrified, thinking how much Mama was counting on the money from the sale of these turkeys and they were all dying! From their hatching time, she had cared for them with great patience and untiring devotion. Baby turkeys are the most helpless creatures known. She had fed them milk curd by hand and sheltered them from predators day and night. The turkeys were really her project and she had made a fine success of raising them.

Faced with deciding what should be done, and without anyone to turn to for advice, the possibility of protecting Mama's interests left only one logical solution. I thought that regardless of their unnatural death the turkeys might still be marketable if we plucked their feathers immediately. Papa had told me feathers were easy to pull while the fowl was warm but set after the body cooled so no time could be lost. We began plucking feathers.

We soon found that body feathers came freely but wing, tail and fringe feathers were difficult. We worked frantically but when I straightened up to observe the turkeys my heart sank because even those that were the cleanest picked looked very unfinished.

The majority of the flock had expired and others were struggling to survive. One big gobbler nearly reeled back into a sitting position, his head drooping limply, and finally passed out right before my eyes. Our task seemed hopeless. We could never expect to pluck them all while their bodies were still warm.

Suddenly we heard the wagon turning in at the gate. We all scurried out of sight. Jessie and I hid in the barn loft where we could watch everything that happened. The big gobbler, the pride of the flock, that had been plucked cleanest of all, rose and staggered directly into the path of the team, and would have been trampled if Papa hadn't stopped the horse in time. I was appalled at seeing that dead turkey alive and walking. What if all of those dead turkeys came back to life? The possibility was as terrifying as the fact that they had died.

Mama and Papa just stared in bewildered astonishment. Their gaze surveyed the demoralized flock and finally rested on the prize spectacle, the gangling twenty-four pound gobbler. With his long, spindling legs carrying a white, bare body he was a gruesome sight. Right back of his head at the top of his long neck was a collar of feathers; in front of his breast was a clump of feathers like a cravat; at the lower end of the drumstick a garter of feathers; and long wing and tail feathers stuck out behind.

Both parents suddenly broke into irrepressible laughter. This was the time for us to make an appearance if there was to be one. Mama threw her arms around her very bewildered seven- and nine-year-old sons. Both Mama and Papa said they were satisfied that those greedy turkeys had gotten drunk on fermenting apples and corn.

The market in town had bargained for the turks, which were to be delivered dressed and ready for the oven the day before Thanksgiving. Our naked birds would require some protection if they were to survive two days and nights of cold weather before time to butcher them. Mama found an old sweater and set about measuring, cutting, and sewing garments for them.

Next morning all of the turkeys had regained their composure and strutted about in their wool pajamas. They all reached Thanksgiving dinner tables.*

I think this writer did a wonderful job of making us see the turkeys. Notice the figures of speech he uses in the tenth paragraph to help us visualize the gobbler. He describes the bird as having a "collar of feathers," a "garter of feathers," and a "clump of feathers like a cravat."

In case you have been out of English class long enough to have forgotten exactly what figures of speech are, "collar of feathers" and "garter of feathers" are metaphors. Webster says a metaphor is "a figure of speech in which a word or phrase literally denoting one kind of object or idea is used in place of another to suggest a likeness." Turkeys, of course, don't actually wear collars or garters, but what a wonderful idea it was to use those words to help us see the location of the gobbler's remaining feathers. "Like a cravat" is a simile, which Webster defines as "a figure of speech comparing two unlike things, often introduced by like or as." You will find the use of metaphors and similes very helpful when you are trying to describe something that you want your readers to be able to visualize.

TWENTY-ONE

Family Traditions

One of my students described a family tradition as "something that sort of slips up on you."

"You don't say, 'Now we're going to start a family tradition,'" he said. "You just go along living your life until suddenly you realize that you have developed some family traditions without knowing it."

Sometimes, too, families have traditions without ever realizing they are traditions. They have activities in which they customarily engage year after year and realize only in retrospect, after the family is grown and scattered, that these activities were indeed cherished traditions. Did you have some such activities in your family, things you took for granted, but the memory of which will last as long as you live? If you do, write them down so that your children and their children can know about them, and so that you, yourself, can have the job of reliving them as you write about them.

Perhaps you are one of my younger readers still in the midst of living with the family traditions in your parents' home, or beginning to build traditions in your own young family. If so, this assignment may cause you to stop and savor the richness of your life as it is right now. This was the case with the young man who wrote the following story:

I hadn't thought about it being a tradition, but Saturday breakfast is a very big deal at our house.

My father's job takes him away a lot, and my two sisters and I have always had lots of activities which kept us busy, too. With all of us rushing around the way we do, there are usually several nights during the week when we don't get to have dinner together as a family. Even when we do all eat together, one of us is usually having to hurry off somewhere.

One thing we always do, though, is have breakfast together on Saturday morning. My mother always fixes an extra nice breakfast, usually bakes muffins or some other kind of special hot bread, or other delicious treat. We all sit around the table and talk and catch up on what everyone has been doing all week.

We never actually agreed that we would all show up at the same time for Saturday morning breakfast. I don't know how it began. I guess it happened to work out a few times and we all enjoyed it and then each one of us just decided to keep that time open for the family. I know I did this once myself when I started taking hockey lessons on Saturday morning. I had a choice of an 8:30 class or a 10:30 class. I chose the 10:30 class even though a lot of my friends were going at 8:30. I just didn't want to miss those breakfasts; so unless it was something pretty special I didn't plan anything much before 10 o'clock on Saturday morning. I wouldn't be surprised if the rest of the family did the same thing and just didn't mention it to the rest of us. Nobody in the family knows why I chose the late hockey class. We have been having these breakfasts for years now, so I guess you would call them a family tradition.

Now that I am away at school those Saturday mornings are the main thing I miss about being away from home, and they are the main thing I look forward to when I go home on vacation. I often wonder if my parents know how much those breakfasts have meant to me all these years. Maybe sometime, if it doesn't seem too sentimental and embarrassing, I'll tell them.

One of my students, a woman in her early forties, started a tradition in her family:

When I was four years old I unwittingly started what I guess could be called a family tradition—winter picnics. We lived on a farm in the Ozarks and had no close neighbors. My only brother, Bob, was eleven and away at school during the day so I always had to devise my own fun.

One very cold morning—my mother says it was fourteen degrees below zero—I decided to go on a picnic. My mother objected strenuously, telling me that people didn't go on picnics in the middle of the winter, that there was snow on the ground, and that a little girl like me couldn't possibly go out in weather like this.

I nagged and nagged until, as I heard my mother tell my father later, "She nearly drove me crazy. I finally decided that the best way to put a stop to the whole thing was to let her go because I was sure she would be back inside in a couple of minutes."

My mother got out my Easter basket and placed a lunch in it for me. Dressed in my snow suit, I started out for my first winter picnic. I found a short stump with about six inches of snow on it, brushed the snow off, sat down, and ate every bite of that basket lunch. I remember sitting all alone on my stump and loving every minute of that cold, snowy picnic.

After that I frequently demanded to be allowed to have winter picnics. One day I talked my mother into going with me, and she thought it was fun, too. We took my sled and played for an hour or so after lunch. Gradually, my brother and my father began to complain about being left out so we started planning winter picnics for the whole family, particularly when there was a lot of nice snow.

We left the farm when I was about six and moved to Albion, Michigan. While I was growing up we didn't have a car and not much money. One of our favorite entertainments was walking to the local park as a family for picnics. My dad was still alive then so these picnics remain some of my happiest memories. In Michigan, winter came early and stayed late, and there was lots of snow. Many times we cooked fried potatoes and hamburgers with so much snow falling we had to cover the frying pans to keep the food dry. Needless to say, we were the only people in the park.

When I got married my husband was still in college, and we were struggling financially. We had a small daughter while he was still in school. Again, picnics were our main family entertainment. We used to go with another couple and I convinced them that we didn't have to stop having picnics just because it got to be late fall and then winter. We used to have wonderful picnics when it was so cold we had to huddle around the fire to keep warm.

One year, after my husband had graduated from college, all of our family gathered at my brother's house in Ohio for Christmas. My brother's family, too, had carried on the tradition of year-around picnics. It was only natural that when we all got together we would plan one of our winter picnics. My Aunt Neen came to spend Christmas with us that year. She is a dedicated city dweller and her idea of roughing it is to turn the thermostat down to 72 degrees. She swears she didn't even go outdoors until she was thirty. She was shocked when we announced that we were going to have a Christmas Eve picnic down by the river. She was a good sport, though, and agreed to go, although she protested all the way that it was the most outrageous thing she had ever heard of.

The river flowed through a deep canyon, and we got there just as the sun was going down. I remember that my aunt looked up at the trees on the side of the hill. Their bare branches were black against the pink of the sunset. She said, "Why, for goodness sake, look how beautiful those bare tree limbs are. It never occurred to me that trees could be beautiful without their leaves, but they are. They are just beautiful in a different way than they are in summer."

I felt very proud of my aunt for noticing the winter beauty. She could have just stood around and shivered and complained, but she didn't. I particularly liked the fact that she noticed the beauty of the bare tree limbs because it reminded me of many times when I was very little. I used to stand all by myself and look up at the bare trees against the sky and think they looked like black lace.

We put up a tarpaulin windbreak, built a big fire, had mugs of hot clam chowder which we had brought from home in a thermos jug, and broiled sausage sandwiches over the fire. That particular Christmas Eve in the snow with our huge fire lighting up that beautiful river canyon has turned out to be a special memory for all of us, including my aunt.

To this day our family is still having winter picnics, and I hope we always will. I can't help feeling a little sorry for people who don't enjoy the outdoors all the year around.

Don't think your family activities have to be as unusual as winter picnics to constitute a tradition worth writing about. When I was in junior high and high school I was the only child left at home and on Sunday night my father always popped corn and I made fudge while my mother wrote letters.

When I went away to school, and later when I was working in Germany, my father and mother continued the corn popping and fudge making. Once when I was in Germany Daddy wrote that his fudge was pretty good but that it wasn't as good as mine. He said that while they missed me all of the time they really missed me on Sunday nights. His letter made me very homesick. I wrote back and said, "I make fudge here, but it isn't as good because Europeans have never heard of black walnuts. I have to settle for English walnuts or pecans." A few weeks later a pint of picked out black walnut meats came through the mail with a note in my father's handwriting which said, "For Your Fudge." A letter from my mother said that from the time my letter about the nuts arrived my dad had spent nearly every evening picking out black walnuts for me. And anyone who has ever struggled to pick out a black walnut knows what a labor of love that was.

Maybe our fudge making and popcorn popping wasn't dignified enough to be labeled a family tradition, but I think those evenings are a memory well worth recording. Don't overlook your small fudge-making, popcorn-popping type memories. They tell a great deal about you and your family.

TWENTY-TWO

Immigrants

Novelist Willa Cather, after she had traveled in many countries in Europe, made the statement that the most cosmopolitan period of her life was when she was a child in the late 1800s living on the Nebraska plains. Her parents' farm was surrounded by the farms of Scandinavians, Bohemians, Spanish, French, and Germans.

She didn't just know these people casually as she might have if she had met them while traveling as a guest in their native lands. They were her friends, she visited in their homes, learned their customs, and she was often invited to celebrate their holidays and national festivals with them. It wasn't at all unusual for her to observe not only the Easter celebrated by most American Christian denominations, but also to celebrate Russian Easter with Orthodox Christian friends. Christmas, too, meant participating in the celebrations of people of many nationalities and she was introduced to many holidays and national festivals with which Americans were unfamiliar.

After she was grown Cather wrote, "On Sunday we could drive to a Norwegian church and listen to a sermon in that language, or to a Danish or Swedish church. We could go to a French Catholic settlement or into the Bohemian township and hear one in Czech or we could go to church with the German Lutherans."

While not all Americans have as rich an experience with new Americans as Willa Cather could claim, the immigration experience is so much a part of our American heritage that stories about immigrants have appeared in nearly all of my classes. Many have been from students who are, themselves, immigrants. Others are from students who are the children or relatives of immigrants. Nearly all Americans know or have known some immigrants well. Many Americans have helped people immigrate from other countries or have helped them settle in the United States once they have arrived.

Some immigrant stories are touching, some are funny, some are inspiring and occasionally one is humiliating. The following story, which I think is both amusing and touching, describes the efforts of a little American boy and his brothers and sisters to Americanize their family:

Everybody loves Thanksgiving Day. It is a nonsectarian holiday with a universal appeal.

My brother, my sisters, and I were born in this country but my parents and all of my relatives immigrated from Eastern Europe. In 1924, when we were small children, we became aware that Thanksgiving was a holiday for everyone. As Jews we celebrated Passover and Chanukah; Christians celebrated Easter and Christmas; but everyone could celebrate Thanksgiving.

At school we learned that our forefathers landed at Plymouth Rock in 1620. It wasn't until we were a little older that we discovered that our own particular forefathers were never anywhere near Plymouth Rock. Our father, in fact, landed at Ellis Island in 1906. Nonetheless, everybody's forefathers came here for the same reasons—either to escape religious persecution or to seek a better life. Anyway, my brothers and sisters and I were native-born Americans and no one could take that away from us.

We learned a song at school that we were told was appropriate for the holiday, but we thought that unless a Thanksgiving dinner was forthcoming, we would have no place to sing it. A concerted effort (incessant pestering, really) by us children resulted in my Aunt Rachel's undertaking the cooking of what was to her an alien feast.

Aunt Rachel, who lived on the Lower East Side of New York, invited my family to join her own in the great venture. We advised her that a turkey would be required. The traditional "fixins" to go with the turkey, we explained, were chestnut stuffing, sweet potatoes, and cranberry sauce. Soup, made from giblets, should precede the main dish, and mince or pumpkin pie should follow. Some cooked vegetables—carrots, peas, green beans, broccoli, or Brussel sprouts—were appropriate for the occasion.

As Aunt Rachel listened to our proposed menu one could almost see her mind working—sorting out those things which would meet the requirements for kashruth (clean in accordance with Jewish ritual law) from those that did not. It was fine, according to Aunt Rachel, to cook what was traditional as long as the laws of kashruth were observed. The first rule is that meat products and dairy products must never be eaten at the same meal. The second rule is never to mix the dishes used for meat products with those used for dairy products. (Included in the term "dishes" are such things as cutlery, pots, pans, containers, and even dish towels, tablecloths, and napkins.) Glass is neutral and can be used with either meat or dairy dishes.

An orthodox Jewish home must have a minimum of four sets of dishes (and cutlery, and so on). One set is for meat and one is for dairy the year around. During the week of Passover, it is forbidden to use the same dishes that were used all year, and so it is necessary to have two different sets of dishes for this holiday.

Thanksgiving arrived. The first course was the soup. Nobody had to teach my Aunt Rachel how to make soup, especially chicken soup. Delicious.

The meal proceeded according to tradition but with variations. The stuffing for the turkey was not cooked inside the bird, but in a baking pan and since my aunt was unfamiliar with chestnuts and the other stuffing ingredients, our stuffing took the form of a kugel (potato pudding)—a forgivable and delightful substitution. The cranberry sauce, equally unfamiliar to my eastern European aunt, became a compote of stewed pears, apples, and cherries. Again a pardonable and delectable stand-in. The reason given for this change was that it was good for the moogen (the digestive tract). A strictly Jewish touch was added to the feast in the form of a tzimmes, a pudding made of sweet potatoes, carrots, prunes, bits of meat, and—I think—honey. So far, everything was fine.

Then the turkey made its appearance at the table. Instead of a roasted, brown, Norman Rockwell fowl there appeared a pale looking bird, hacked into eighths or sixteenths and boiled. No one had told Aunt Rachel that it was supposed to be roasted whole.

"Roasted?" my aunt asked. "I cooked it! How else could I make chicken soup?"

I guess that to my aunt, a turkey was a big chicken, and a chicken had one ultimate aim in life, to become chicken soup. The stewed turkey did not taste as good as it would have tasted if it had been roasted, but you have to give Aunt Rachel "E" for effort even if not for excellence.

That first Thanksgiving dinner took place a long time ago. Aunt Rachel, my parents, indeed all of my family except my sister Molly and me, are long gone. As new Americans we may not have had too much in common with the Southerners, the Westerners, or the New Englanders, but on that particular day we felt we were one with all of them when we sang, as we were sure they were doing, the song we had learned in school, "We gather together to ask the Lord's blessing."*

The next immigrant story is a sad one about a shameful chapter in American history, but shameful or not it is part of our history and therefore should not be forgotten. There is so much to be proud of in America's past that I feel that those of us who have been involved in, or have seen first hand, American unfairness or lack of wisdom have a responsibility to write about that part of the American experience as we are to write about American generosity, ingenuity, and the like. This story is about one of the Japanese-American citizens who was held in a detention camp during World War II which was, of course, a violation of his constitutional rights.

The tree still stands gnarled and beautiful. I remember the day in 1942 when Kogi planted it. It was the last time I saw him. He was alighting from his gardening truck carrying a plant, just a usual, peaceful event. That this day would be different, I had no clue.

"Miss Detweiler, can I leave this peach tree here? It's from my ancestors," he said.

"Of course, Kogi, but don't you want it at your house?"

"There is no house. They say I am not a good citizen."

"I don't understand, Kogi."

"It's in the paper. We Japanese-American citizens are dangerous aliens. We can't stay here. Tomorrow I go to Pomona and probably Wyoming or Colorado to a prison camp. Prison camp for me, Miss Detweiler.

"Yuki and Joe will go to prison camp with me." I knew Kogi's wife was dead and that he had a daughter about ten and a son who was eight.

I stepped into the house and called my father to say goodbye to Kogi. Dad was Swiss and was much slandered during World War I because he was considered German. We three shook hands tearfully, father doubtlessly reliving the past. Words were difficult.

"Oh, Kogi, the tree!" I said, "I don't know anything about bonsai."

Kogi had started for his gardening truck. He came back with a shovel.

"I put it here," he said, choosing a bright corner by the back door.

"Water once a week. Is good fruit. When I come back, I get. OK?"

"Of course, Kogi. I'm so sorry. Can I do anything?"

"The church has our things. Tomorrow we go. I write; not write good."

He never wrote.

In the spring the tree produced gorgeous, deep pink blossoms that looked so young among the gnarled branches. The peaches were few and since we couldn't bear to eat them we gave them to a neighbor.

The months passed. The tree thrived. It loved the spot Kogi had chosen. The second year we ate the fruit.

At long last the war was over. We awaited Kogi's return but there was no word.

One day a slender, beautiful Asian girl appeared at our door.

"Excuse me," she said, "I'm looking for someone who might have known my father. He was the gardener, Kogi."

"Yuki! Are you Yuki?"

"Yes, yes, you must have known him! I'm trying to find the lady who has the family bonsai tree."

"Yuki! What about your father?"

"Poor father. He died in the camp. He despaired so because of being confined. They were such hard days for us. Father tried carving little wooden birds to keep busy. We loved playing with all the children but sometimes we'd come into the room laughing and joking and abruptly stop when we saw the deep sadness on father's face as he sat carving his little birds. Excuse me," she said tearfully. "I still cry when I remember. Now, about the tree . . ."

We went around in back of the house and Yuki dropped down on her knees by the peach tree while I went to the garage for a shovel.

Yuki had risen to her feet when I joined her by the tree. "I'm sorry it took me so long to come," she said. "It wasn't until recently when I went through his few things that I found the addresses of his customers. Oh, I'm so glad to have found the tree."

"Shall we dig it up now?"

"Oh, no, never!" exclaimed Yuki. "It's happy here. Father planted it here and here it shall stay."

"Yuki, I feel so sad that we let this happen to all of you. Come back any time to see the tree."

TWENTY-THREE

Your Stories Don't Actually Have to Be "Stories"

Many of the stories in this book and that students have written for my classes have been about an incident that had a beginning, a middle, and an end, much like a short story. Sometimes they have been about one person—a sort of character study. However, many students have come up with very creative ideas and have written pieces that told a great deal about their lives but that, in the true sense of the word, could not be called stories. I suppose they might be called essays, but whatever they should be called, they are very interesting. I am including a couple of examples of this kind of story and hope they will spark some ideas for you.

We had a terrible drought in Kansas City while I was teaching a class in the summer of 1980. This reminded one of my students of three other droughts that she remembered and she wrote the following:

The summer of 1980, a terrible drought came to the Midwest with more than a month of over 100 degree days and with the temperature sometimes soaring to 110. Every stone, asphalt pavement, and piece of wood absorbed the heat and it didn't even cool at night. Tasseling corn dried before the moist pollen could fall to the ear and leaves on other plants withered and dropped to the ground. Many shrubs, plants, and even trees died.

People with air conditioning at their work places hurried home to cooled houses or swimming pools, but others without these cooling devices used fans or did without. In Kansas City 168 people died. Some were young workers who did not recognize the symptoms of heat prostration and stayed in the sun too long, but most people who lost their lives were the old, poor, ill, and alone. Often the fear of expense kept them from using fans or air conditioners (if they had them) and fear of burglary kept them from opening their windows. There were cool public places available but many did not have anyone to help them go to one of these refuges or did not want to leave home because of their pets or because they were afraid of being robbed while they were away.

My husband and I took each day at a time, tried not to get too hot, and watered flowers, vegetables, shrubs, trees, and at times the chimneys on our house and the foundation. (We had learned during a previous drought that there is danger that the dry and cracked earth can cause chimneys to lean and foundations to break.)

We sympathized with the farmers who were losing their year's earnings because of the drought. My husband and I had grown up on farms and remembered the fears of our parents as the lack of rain began to cause the loss of crops and of our income for the year. The tension of those bright, brassy days on the farm was terrible. My husband remembered his father getting so angry that he would shake his fist at the sky and shout obscenities at God because He didn't make it rain. My parents, on the other hand, wilted with fear and anguish.

There was another drought in 1956 when the thermometer didn't go below 110 for fourteen days and it was a miserable time, but the drought that nearly devastated the Midwest was the great drought of 1936. There were practically no air conditioned buildings then, just a few movie theaters and some parts of hospitals. We had one twelve-inch fan that we used to try to keep our three-and seven-year-old children cool enough to take their afternoon rest. We wouldn't let them play in the sun and we sometimes had them play in the bathtub for hours.

Electric refrigerators were not common then. We put an ice card in the window that told the iceman what size cake of ice we needed and he would struggle in with a fifty or one hundred-pound cake on his back and deposit it in the ice box. This was the year that followed other dry years and the great dust storms of the 1930s which almost ruined my husband and my parents, and did ruin many other farmers. For several years after this drought with the accompanying dust storms people crossing Oklahoma and Kansas reported being able to see only the tops of fence posts because the rest of the post was buried in dust.

The year of 1913 was another terrible drought year with heat above 100 degrees. I was six years old and my brother, Floyd, was three. We lived in a small house in Hutchinson, Kansas. I remember being sick on a pallet of quilts on the floor near an open door. My father was fanning me and my mother put cool compresses on my forehead. When they found I had measles they moved me to a darkened room to save my eyes and I remember being so sick and so hot. Soon my brother was moved into the dark room also. It wasn't long before we began coughing and coughing. The doctor said we now had whooping cough along with the measles, both diseases dangerous to small children.

The heat was terrible and there were no electric fans and no refrigeration and only a little ice from the ice wagons that came around. We coughed and coughed and sometimes after a coughing spell poor Floyd would lose all he had eaten.

We would not or could not eat very much. My parents tried without success to coax us to taste a new product that had just come on the market—corn flakes. I remember that once my mother went to an ice cream wagon with her plate and brought back three pink mounds of ice-cream. We grew so thin that when a man with a camera came to the door my parents had our picture taken even though money was very scarce because they were afraid we would die.

Notice how the writer managed to recreate the stifling atmosphere of the droughts and how well she describes people's helplessness against heat and drought in 1913 and even in 1980 if they lacked money to protect themselves. The next story, unlike the previous one, is a joyous story. Again, it is more a creative idea than the telling of an actual story but that makes it no less interesting. I think it is an important story because it captures a world that, for many American children, no longer exists.

My wife and I have never been able to convince our grandchildren that we had fun when we were growing up in spite of the fact that we didn't have television. I'm sure there must have been lots of times when we came in the house whining, "Mom, there's nothing to do." But I can't remember them.

When I was a kid in St. Louis we didn't watch. We played. Sidewalks were for playing. Streets were for playing. Alleys were for playing. Steps were for playing. We'd play for hours bouncing a rubber ball up against a house's wooden or concrete steps which led up to the porch. If the ball hit on a step corner and you caught it when it bounced back you got two points; skip it from the step to the riser and catch it and you got one point; miss it and you lost your turn.

Then there were our caves. The neighborhood had a number of vacant lots. At least once each summer we'd all borrow shovels, picks, and spades. We always said we dug caves six feet deep but looking back, since none of us were much over four feet, we were exaggerating. Then we'd find some old boards or corrugated metal to cover the excavation. We dug a hole at the side so we could crawl in and out. In the side of the cave we'd dig out a space for a fire and insert an old piece of stovepipe. Then we'd smuggle potatoes out of the house under our coats and bake them. The potatoes always burned to a crisp on the outside, never got done on the inside, and seldom were eaten.

Spring brought out the marbles. You saved up your money to buy an agate for a shooter. Or you looked for a steel ball bearing which would really send the marbles flying out of the circle.

On hot August days, we found a shady spot and played mumblety-peg. You played it with a pocket knife, the object of the game being to make the knife stick in the ground by using different maneuvers. Each time you made the knife stand up you got to try again until you missed. Every maneuver had a name. For example, "stab the butcher" was started by laying the knife along the fingernails of your right clenched fist, the blade pointing up. Turn your fist down with a little thrust and the knife should stick. Then the left fist. Somehow I don't remember anyone being hurt playing what was, of course, a dangerous game.

And there was sandstone. We colored white sand with bluing, red ink, black ink, and anything else we could think of. We'd sell the colored sand to other kids for straight pins and safety pins. Sometimes the white sand would be alternated with layers of colored sand into a catsup bottle or small jelly jar to make a rainbow.

Warm nights when there wasn't any school are the most memorable. A gas light was on our side of the street, in the middle of the block. When supper was over (the evening meal was always called supper) the kids would gather in front of the gas lamp. That is, all except the older boys, who met at the side door of Brennan's. We moved out of the neighborhood before I was old enough to find what they did.

But back at the Oakland Avenue gas lamp there was plenty of action. Toward dusk the lamp lighter would come up the street, carrying a long pole with a light on the end against his shoulder. We'd keep our distance while he lit the lamp. Then we'd start.

There were games played on the steps. In rock school all players but one would sit on the bottom step. The one who was IT would hold a pebble in one of his or her clenched fists, hold out both hands and the first player guessed which hand held the rock. If the guess was right, he or she moved up one step. Then the next player would guess. The first one to get to the top step became IT.

There were sidewalk games. One was called lemonade with a rhyme that went: "Lemonade, lemonade. Tell me your name and I'll tell you my trade." I don't remember the rest of the game. Run-sheep-run was another one.

The girls played hopscotch, jacks, and skipping rope and everybody played hide and seek and tag. At nine o'clock the curfew at Liggett & Myers Tobacco Co. would sound. That meant all the kids had to go home.

When we were about ten or eleven and could "leave the block," some of the guys would walk up to Kings Highway on warm summer evenings and ride the dinky (a small streetcar that could operate in either direction by reversing the trolley pole). The dinky ran on Kings Highway to connect two main streetcar lines. The dinky required no transfers and charged no fares.

When it got dark we'd creep under the bushes in Forest Park trying to spy on a couple doing what they shouldn't be doing. Then we'd wonder what it was exactly that they were doing. Knowledge of sex was a little blurry at our age in those days.

When snow covered Forest Park, the most popular hill for sledding was (and still is) Art Hill, but it was too crowded. Our favorite hill was the Royal Bump, which was a deep, narrow, twisting path leading downward to the River Des Peres, an open sewer. It took skill to steer a sled without hitting a tree, flipping over, or, the ultimate fate to be avoided, winding up in that river.

In 1926, the Cardinals won their first pennant. That made playing baseball the most popular game in town. We'd play catch in the alley or on the street. Forest Park, with its ball diamonds, was only a few blocks away. We'd play against teams from other neighborhoods and the umpire was a substitute on one of the teams. Our games were fun and completely unsupervised. You never saw an adult at a kid's game, except one of the Forest Park bums.

Think what we would have missed if we had had television!*

You can see from reading these two stories that you can sometimes put together a composite of memories and ideas and create a very interesting chapter for your book.

TWENTY-FOUR

Brief Encounters

One day near the end of the semester one of my students who had written some marvelous stories for the class said, "Well, I couldn't think of anything more to write about any of the assignments this week so I made up an assignment that I call "Brief Encounters." Here is how his story began:

As I have been writing about my life for this class I have remembered many very brief, sometimes only momentary, encounters that I have had with people that I had never met before and will never meet again but with whom I was involved in some sort of a "happening." These encounters give wonderful spice to one's life and can later be remembered and savored.

What a wonderful idea! The student then followed the above introduction with sixteen widely varied encounters, none of which lasted more than a few minutes. They ranged from an amusing encounter with a woman in the checkout line at the supermarket to his being scolded by a janitor in an art gallery. Some were funny, some sad, and some embarrassing. Here are two of them:

Once when I was on a trip to Paris I had been having trouble with my leg and was having a hard time walking. I decided I needed a cane to help me get around. Where does one buy a cane in Paris when one does not speak French? I tried different places with no luck until I came to a menswear store where I found a young clerk who spoke a little English. She told me to go to a place that sold artificial limbs. Then she added, "I zink ze gentleman should know zat ze cane is no longer in good style in Paris."

The student's second brief encounter took place in Africa during World War II:

One night I worked late at the depot in Tunis. On the way back to my billet I almost ran over an English soldier who leaped out in front of my Jeep. I stopped and he came over and said, "Old chap, there is something bloody queer going on in that alley and I need a little help."

I got out of the jeep and listened. There were screams of pain. With a flashlight we soon discovered that a man was trying to take his wife somewhere and that she was in labor and about to have a baby in that dark alley. The husband and the Englishman and I jerked a door off a bomb damaged building. We placed our jackets on the door and soon had the woman on the improvised litter and loaded into the jeep.

Although there was a blackout in Tunis, I turned on my lights and kept the horn blowing. The Englishman and the husband held onto the woman and at every bump she screamed and the Englishman cursed. All of this soon attracted the attention of the military police.

Suspecting foul play, they pulled their revolvers, stopped us, and demanded an explanation. With the Englishman and husband giving advice and the poor woman screaming, I managed to explain the situation to the MPs who finally conducted us to the hospital with dispatch. This really ended this brief encounter except that I checked later at the hospital and learned from the excited new father that he "thought" the baby was born in the jeep on the way to the hospital. The mother and baby were doing fine and they had named the little boy Jeep. So somewhere in Tunis today there is a middle-aged man whose name is Jeep.

As he read about his brief encounters, some of my own long-forgotten brief encounters ran through my mind. I know the same thing was happening with people in the class because several of them were nodding, smiling, and jotting down notes all of the time he was reading.

One brief encounter that I remembered occurred when I was about seven or eight years old. I was visiting my aunt and uncle who lived on a farm. My aunt was in the habit of putting new clothes on their scarecrow every spring because the winter weather had almost demolished the clothes he had worn the previous summer. She had washed a pair of my uncle's old coveralls and one of his discarded shirts and we went out to dress the scarecrow. When we got through he looked quite respectable.

A few hours later, while we were eating lunch, there was a knock at the kitchen door. My aunt opened it and there stood a hobo. He tipped his hat and asked politely, "Excuse me, ma'am. Would you mind if I changed clothes with your scarecrow?"

Give some thought to writing about your brief encounters and slip some into your story. They will give your readers wonderful glimpses of your everyday life. They may give them a laugh or like this next story, they may make them shed a tear or two. It's a brief encounter that occurred nearly eighty years ago but has remained in the writer's memory all of these years.

When I was five or six years old, my widowed father and my sister and brother and I were traveling west in a covered wagon. When we reached eastern Arizona we stopped in at a place called the Land of the Navajo. There I met a little Indian girl my age caring for her old blind grandmother and grandfather. Their wikiup was very small and they cooked on a stone fireplace. I made friends with the little girl and I let her hold my doll. It had been made of wood by a Mexican man and his wife had made it a dress. It was the only doll I ever owned. I thought it was beautiful and loved it dearly.

The Indian girl's name was Nickino. She also loved my doll and wanted to put it on her back. I couldn't speak her language but in signs I said, "No—in your arms. Say, 'Bye, baby, bye.'" She was smart and caught on quick.

When we got ready to move on she wanted to keep my lovely doll. I said, "No, mine!"

She cried and my sister said, "Give her the doll."

"I can't," I said, "I love her."

My sister said, "She has nothing and you have me and brother and father. All she has is two blind grandparents."

So with tears in my eyes I gave Nickino my Mary. She rocked it in her arms and said, "Bye, baby, bye. Mine." As we drove away she was smiling and waving good-bye to us. Tears were running down her little brown cheeks.

My sister put her arms around me and said, "You will always remember this day." I have. And I often wonder what became of the three Indians.*

More Living, More Stories

There is really no place to end this book. It could go on and on. There are several categories on the assignment list which I haven't covered, but if I included a chapter on every assignment we would have to double the size of the book. Besides, I'm afraid you would spend too much time reading and not enough time writing! I have included enough information and samples to give you an idea of how it all works, and you will get many more ideas as you read other people's autobiographies.

There's another problem with trying to end this book. The assignment list continues to grow even as I write. When I started teaching the course I had an assignment list of about twenty categories. You will note that there are now many more on the list. One of these categories—food—has been added since I started writing this book.

A young woman in one of my workshops had recently been appointed associate administrator of a nursing home which had all black patients and an all-black staff. She and the administrator were the only white people in the home. She wrote:

The food was exceptionally well cooked and not nearly as institutional as in other homes where I have worked. But after I had been there a few weeks I noticed that the lunches the employees brought from home included many dishes which might be classified as "soul food." They brought greens, cornbread, sweet potato pie, and more.

I asked the cook whether this was the kind of food the residents would have been accustomed to eating at home. She said it was, and I asked, "Well, why don't we serve some of these dishes? I would certainly hate to know that I was going to spend the rest of my life someplace where I could never again taste some of my favorite foods." The cook said it would be fine with her if it was all right with the dietitian.

The dietitian, also white, was a consultant who came in once a month to help with any problems and to bring our menus for the next month. She was delighted with the idea, said she had never before had to work any kind of ethnic foods into an institutional menu, and thought it would be an interesting challenge. She and I asked the cook to take us to the best soul food restaurant in town so we could see exactly what kind of food we were talking about. She took us to a wonderful restaurant where we did our best to eat our way through the menu.

Then we passed out questionnaires to the residents asking them to write the names of favorite foods they were missing and would like to have included in the menu. You can't imagine with what enthusiasm the residents responded. (There isn't much excitement in a nursing home and when you have an idea that really generates some interest among the residents, it gives you a wonderful feeling.)

Our menus are now sprinkled with soul food, some of it cooked from recipes supplied by the residents themselves.

The student who wrote this story actually wrote it for the assignment on "The Accomplishment of Which You Are the Most Proud." However, the class discussion which followed was not about accomplishments but about food—favorite recipes from home, from grandparents' homes, from native lands, and more. We decided that we should add food to our list of assignments and urge students to include in their books favorite family recipes which might otherwise be lost.

I mentioned this new food category to my sister, Lillian. She thought a moment and then said hesitantly, "I have a book that I have been keeping for a long time but I have never shown it to anyone because I was afraid people would think I was silly. I wonder if you would like to look at it."

She brought out a book which she had been keeping for twenty years. It included the dates of all of the luncheons, brunches, dinner parties, and open houses that she had hosted in all that time. It also had the names of all of the guests, and a complete menu of each affair with the name of the cookbook from which each recipe was taken. What a gold mine—and she almost didn't show it to me! Once again let me remind you to talk about what you are doing when you work on your life story, and ask questions even of the most unlikely persons. You never know where help is waiting for you.

One assignment which I haven't covered is "How You Survived the Depression." I want to recommend a book to you which is bound to remind you of one depression story after another if you happen to be one of those who lived through the depression. It is Studs Terkel's *Hard Times: An Oral History of the Great Depression*. It has hundreds of first-person stories about the depression, some of them only one paragraph long, others several pages long.

There are funny stories, tragic stories, stories of generosity and kindness, and stories of selfishness and greed. A similar book about Canadians who survived the depression is *Ten Lost Years, 1929–1939* by Barry Broadfoot. I am sure you will find one or both of these books in your public library.

While I am talking about the depression there is another book which I want especially to recommend to you. It is *Growing Up* by

Russell Baker. While it isn't specifically about the depression it has several chapters about that era. This book wasn't out yet when the first edition of *How to Write Your Own Life Story* was published so I couldn't recommend it then, but I want to say that it is one of the best books you can possibly read to help you with your autobiography. Russell Baker has the wonderful ability to make the smallest, day-to-day events interesting. I urge you to read it right after you read Grandma Moses' book. I still put her book first as a help for the inexperienced writer who is writing an autobiography because of the way it is broken up in small sketches that are easy to manage. But by all means read *Growing Up*.

Subjects which I haven't covered in this book produced stories as interesting as those I have covered. The assignment on "The Influence of the Performing Arts in Your Life" evoked similar and interesting responses from two people in their middle fifties—one a man and one a woman. Both spoke of having been lonely children who spent a great deal of time at the movies in the early 1930s. Both said they felt that the glib, unrealistic, happy-ending movies of that period had had a negative effect on their lives; the inexperienced chorus girl who became a star overnight; the young couple who got married and lived happily ever after; the couple who met, hated each other at first, and then in one blinding flash realized they were in love.

"They gave me a totally unrealistic picture of life," wrote the woman. "I expected life to be like the movies. When it wasn't, I didn't know what to do about it. I missed a lot of good opportunities, both in connection with a career and in connection with my social life, because the situation in which I found myself wasn't the way I thought it should be. I suppose this makes me sound rather stupid, but I have heard other people who grew up on 1930s movies say the same thing."

I'm sure you have had many special moments in your life which you can write about for the "Special Moments" assignment. One example of a special moment was written by a young Pole who immigrated to the United States. He wrote a touching story about his last sight of his Polish village.

Don't let the fact that I haven't written a chapter about a specific assignment keep you from writing about it. Just let your mind wander freely about each topic, keep reading published autobiographies, and then write your own stories.

TWENTY-SIX

Where Do You Live?
Where *Did* You Live?

Carl Nelson of Whittier, California, who uses my book to teach classes in life story writing, sent me an article he reads to his classes. In the article Don Coldsmith, a popular western fiction writer, describes speaking to a high school class near his Kansas ranch. One student raised her hand and asked, "If your books are so successful, why do you live *here?*" Coldsmith said he realized that the girl wasn't asking a question. She was making a statement. She was saying, "Nothing ever happened here, and it's not going to. When I can, I'm leaving."

Coldsmith was sympathetic, knowing most of us feel that way as teenagers, no matter where we grow up, but he wanted people from his part of the country to be able to tell their children and grandchildren the fabulous stories of what had happened in the center of their home state of Kansas. He took a compass and with the center at his ranch drew a circle with a two hundred mile radius. Then he made a list of all of the historic events that occurred inside that circle. "It *all* happened here," he said, "the story of the great American West."

The cowboy legend was born there with the men and boys who worked the great cattle drives from Texas to railheads in central Kansas. The early rodeos began inside the circle.Colorful figures frequented the area: Bat Masterson, Wild Bill Hickok, Doc Holliday, Wyatt Earp, Calamity Jane, Belle Starr, Jim Bridger, Jedediah Smith, Jim Beckwourth, and Kit Carson, to name only a few. The Santa Fe Trail passed near Coldsmith's ranch. The Smoky Hill Trail to the Colorado gold rush cut straight across Kansas and, for awhile, so did the Butterfield Stage. The original Little House on the Prairie was only a few miles from Coldsmith's ranch.

Within an hour's drive of his home, Civil War guerrillas, including Jesse and Frank James and William Quantrill, terrorized the countryside. In nearby Coffeyville, three blocks from the house where Coldsmith grew up, there are bullet holes in the wall of a hardware store made by the guns of the Dalton gang when they were wiped out trying to rob both of the town's banks at the same time. Bonnie and Clyde robbed banks inside the circle.

This is only part of Coldsmith's list.

Of course, not every place has a past as colorful as Coldsmith's circle, but *something* happened *everywhere*, and the place where you live, lived, or were born, is part of your heritage. A little bit of research might provide a very interesting chapter for your story.

A woman in one of my classes whose husband worked for a large chain of retail stores had lived in several cities because her husband was transferred every three or four years as he climbed the corporate ladder. She wrote local histories for three of the towns in which she had lived and included them in her book. Here is part of one of her histories.

I never really felt like I was part of the community in the first two places we lived. By the time we really got acquainted with the city and its people, it was time to move on.

Our third move was to Council Bluffs, Iowa. I had never been west of the Mississippi, and I expected my Council Bluffs years to be very dreary. I was wrong. While living there I developed a hobby that I have pursued in each place we have lived since. Instead of moping around feeling sorry for myself, I spent three fascinating years researching Council Bluffs history.

It started when we had been in town only a couple of weeks. I happened to drive past the Bloomer School. The word "bloomer" caught my eye and brought back miserable child- hood memories. When I went to a country school near Mount Carroll, Illinois, my mother made me wear black sateen bloomers in the winter. She said they were warm and didn't show the dirt. You can't imagine how ugly they were. I dreaded for fall to come because I had to start wearing them. I hated them! My pain was lessened only slightly by the fact that all of the other girls in my school had to wear them too—with one exception. Doris lived on a farm like the rest of us, but it was a chicken farm with a big hatchery, and her parents were rich. She wore beautiful little crepe panties called step-ins. They had lace around the legs and buttoned at the waist. Oh, how the rest of us envied her.

I hadn't thought of those hideous black bloomers for years, but I remembered them each time I passed Bloomer School. Finally, I asked a woman in my Sunday School class how the school got its name.

"I'm not sure," she said, "but I think it was named for Amelia Bloomer—you know, the woman who invented the bloomer."

Why on earth, I wondered, would they name a school for a woman who had inflicted such misery on little girls? I decided to go to the library and see what I could find out about her.

Amelia and Dexter Bloomer, who had been happily married for fifteen years, arrived in Council Bluffs by stage at five o'clock on the evening of April 15, 1855. (Kit Carson was also a passen- ger on the stage.) Both Amelia and Dexter left successful publishing careers behind in the East. Dexter had been editor and publisher of the weekly *Western Home Visitor* in Mount Vernon, Ohio. Amelia had been editor and publisher of *The Lily*, a feminist/temperance paper, which had wide national circulation. Both Amelia and Dexter played an important role in Council Bluffs history.

I found out that Amelia didn't invent the bloomer. It was designed by Elizabeth Miller. While on her honeymoon in Switzerland, Elizabeth visited a sanitarium for women recuperating from respiratory problems brought on by *the effects of the tight-lacing that the fashion of the day required and by lack of physical exercise.* (Italics added.) She noticed what comfortable clothes the women were wearing and decided to have a similar outfit made for traveling. She wore long, full Turkish trousers of black broadcloth gathered in at the ankle. Over the trousers she wore a dress with a short skirt that reached just below the knee. Her husband approved of her outfit and defended his pioneering wife against all criticism.

Her cousin, Elizabeth Cady Stanton of Senaca Falls, New York, later wrote that she became convinced that there was need for reform in women's dress when she saw her cousin with a lamp in one hand and the latest Stanton baby in the other, walk up a flight of stairs with ease and grace. She, on the other hand, was struggling to pull herself and her flowing skirt and five petticoats up the stairs while carrying a can of hot water. She promptly made herself a costume like Elizabeth Miller's.

Dressed in their new outfits, the two cousins went to call on Amelia Bloomer, who also lived in Seneca Falls at the time. Amelia thought the costume was very sensible and had a similar one made for herself and wrote about it in *The Lily.* She told her readers that she and her friends made their dresses with a loose and easy waist and without whalebone, saying that being able to breathe deeply and freely was the most glorious part of wearing the costume.

Amelia had no intention of setting a new style, certainly not of having it named for her, but the fame of both the new costume and Amelia spread rapidly. Letters asking for patterns poured into *The Lily* from women anxious to throw off the burden of their layers of heavy skirts.

Plays and musicals were written about what everybody was calling "Bloomerism." Newspapers and magazines featured it, and top designers created beautiful variations of it. There were Bloomer balls, the Bloomer Polka, the Bloomer Waltz, the Bloomer Schottisch, and the Bloomer Quadrille.

The Bloomer costume turned out to be a great asset to the early feminist movement. In the United States, England, and France, the fad brought many invitations to women to lecture about the practicality of the costume. These speakers were all ardent supporters of the emancipation of women and used their frequent speaking invitations to press for equal rights for women. These highly intelligent, often witty, women provided much of the education for both men and women that laid the groundwork for the passage many decades later of the constitutional amendment that gave women the right to vote.

Amelia and Dexter left their friends and their careers in the East to move to Council Bluffs simply because they wanted to. The West called, and like so many other citizens of the restless young country, they answered. At first, Dexter thought he might set up a newspaper. However, since he was a lawyer and there was a great need for legal work in connection with the many land transactions occurring in the area where new settlers were pouring in, he decided to practice law. He also became a leader in an effort to establish a public school system for Council Bluffs. In fact, he was often referred to as "the father of the city's school system." (Bloomer School was named for him, not for Amelia.)

To her surprise, when Amelia arrived in Council Bluffs she found that her fame as a speaker had preceded her, and she began receiving invitations to speak almost immediately. The first one was from the pastor of the Congregationalist church who offered her his pulpit to speak about education for women. One successful speaking engagement led to another, and she was even invited to speak before the Iowa and Nebraska legislatures. She had rigorous speaking tours throughout Iowa, Nebraska, and Kansas.

The example set by Amelia's pioneering in the rugged West encouraged other feminists to do the same. Amelia's home became the stopping place for women who embarked on long, arduous propaganda tours under primitive conditions in all kinds of weather. Council Bluffs became a hub for feminist activities with speakers who were staying at Amelia's home fanning out into three states. She was responsible for the establishment of the Women's Suffrage Society of Iowa and became its first president. In 1880, all of the trustees of the Council Bluffs Public Library were women.

She temporarily abandoned her work on behalf of women during the Civil War. She and Dexter were ardent abolitionists, and their house became the headquarters for all the Council Bluffs organizations working for the welfare of the men of the Union Army. She and the women who worked with her sent a constant flow of warm clothing and hospital supplies to the front. Her efforts were so outstanding that General Ulysses S. Grant, commander of the Union armies, asked to meet her and thank her for setting so fine an example. After the war she received letters from many men saying that because of what she had done for the soldiers they would now support suffrage for women.

Amelia died on December 31, 1893, and is buried in Fair View Cemetery on a hill above Council Bluffs.

I was so excited about all I was finding out about Amelia that I babbled about her wherever I went and was surprised and disappointed to discover how many people of Council Bluffs had no idea who she was.

I never found any connection between "Bloomerism" and my black sateen bloomers, but I feel sure of one thing. Amelia would have thought them a disgrace since she was always feminine and loved pretty clothes and wanted all women to have them. I am positive she would have fought for my right to wear step-ins!

My student also wrote about the fact that Council Bluffs got its name because it was built on bluffs overlooking the Missouri River where the first meeting between Native North Americans and French fur traders was held. She wrote about the Rogers and Clark expedition passing the bluffs, but most of her story about Council Bluffs history focused on Amelia Bloomer.

Incidentally, I don't think we should think too badly of the people of Council Bluffs for not knowing about Amelia. I'm sorry to say that we Americans often ignore not only our personal history and family history, but also the history of the towns, states, and even the country that nurtured us. A recent example of this occurred last year when my niece was visiting from Oregon. She and I drove out to Independence, ten miles from Kansas City where I now live. We were walking around the neighborhood where we both grew up when she stopped suddenly in front of a large old house on the corner of River and Waldo streets. "Why, I didn't know that!" she exclaimed. She was reading a plaque that had recently been placed in front of the house. "I came here every week for two years for my dramatic class when I was in the fifth and sixth grades, and nobody ever told me that this is the house where Harry Truman grew up."

I might add that although I have spent most of my life in Independence and Kansas City, until I became editor first of *Westport Magazine* and later of the *Overland Journal*, I was only dimly aware of the role Independence and Westport (now part of Kansas City) played in the opening of the West. Let's help recapture our history whenever we can.

TWENTY-SEVEN

They Read
the Book and
Got Busy!

*I*n the introduction to this book I wrote about how gratifying it has
been to me to receive letters and telephone calls from people telling me they are not just *reading* the book but are actually *writing*.
Some people have even sent me stories they have written. Now that
the book has been out sixteen years and I am working on the fourth
edition, there has been ample time for me to get a lot of feedback
and to realize that the book is being used extensively to assist people
in writing their stories. In this chapter I want to tell you about two
men who have used it, each in a different way. Both are World War II
veterans, each wrote about a phase of the war that hasn't been widely
publicized.

One of my speeches about the book was attended by a woman
whose name is Ivanelle Manning. She bought several copies of the
book and sent one to her brother, Chester Garthwait of Fennimore,
Wisconsin. She said he had had a very interesting life, and she had
been trying for years to get him to write about it. A couple of years
later she sent me a copy of the book he wrote. She said, "He read
your book straight through and went right out and bought a notebook and started writing." Chester had several hundred copies of

the book printed for his family, friends, and neighbors, and for people mentioned in the book. Needless to say, I was thrilled to receive the book, and I'm thrilled now to be able to share some very brief excerpts from it with you.

Chester majored in agriculture in college. His agricultural education included training in surveying, which gave him an excellent background for serving in the 612 Graves Registration Company. He was a T/Sgt and headed a cemetery survey unit during much of the war. Please don't avoid reading his story because you fear reading about graves might be depressing. It is a sad story, of course, but since 252,084 Americans died on the battlefields of Europe, you can imagine what an important job Chester had taking care of daily deaths. It is also interesting and somewhat heartening to read about the care with which the Army handled the bodies and identification of our casualties.

Because of space limitations I have had to omit much fascinating information from his World War II chapter, such as his friendship with several French families and his shock when his own cousin was brought in for burial. Incidentally, after the war Chester served as a pallbearer at his cousin's funeral after his body was returned to his family in the States.

Here are parts of his story:

The negative factors about serving in a Graves Registration Company were that cemeteries were not needed unless soldiers were being killed, so we would be operating near the front. We were going to have to deal with severe psychological problems and probably would never be heroes, but we were to perform an extremely sensitive service.

Twenty-six days after D day we marched with full packs from Omaha Beach. Tom Piper took some pictures that were later used in our company history. A few years ago, *Time* magazine's feature on World War II used one of those photographs, and my son-in-law recognized my picture thirty-five years later.

Our first home in France was near the little town of Isigny. We could hear the noise of big guns and strafing planes. I was sent to do some work in the first American cemetery, St. Laurent. Four thousand servicemen were removed from the English Channel and beaches for immediate burial there. Later it would become a permanent burial ground and be enlarged to thirty-seven acres. This is the cemetery President Jimmy Carter would later accept as a tribute from France.

The St. Laurent is one of six permanent American cemeteries in Europe. As the various fronts moved forward, fifty-four temporary cemeteries were created. Chester worked on thirty-four of them, plus laying out a couple of cemeteries for Displaced Persons Camps.

Chester describes the need for meticulous surveying. At one point during the war he visited a cemetery he had laid out months before and saw proof of how important it was that cemeteries and graves be measured correctly and exact records and blueprints completed:

A military transport glider had been cut loose by enemy fire and skidded diagonally through the cemetery. The markers were thrown several hundred yards and were in complete disarray. What if our measurements and blueprints had not been precise, showing the exact position and name for each grave? It is possible that the wrong body would have been sent home for civilian burial. (Later, our company received recognition for having a 97.7 percent "positive identification" record. Considering the number of fragmented bodies, this was excellent.)

●

The first cemetery I laid out was St. Mere Eglise. American dead were buried in one segment and enemy dead in another.

At this time there were no Allied dead in the area. We were sleeping in double foxholes because there was still considerable strafing of the area. We were terrorized at night by anti-aircraft cannon frequently set up behind hedgerows near us.

Our company was designated early as an Advance Section Unit, which was a flattering evaluation of the quality of our service, but it meant we would have to operate near the front. Other units with a less favorable rating would beautify established cemeteries and bury deceased patients from hospitals. Also they handled bodies that were later found in searches called "screening the area" for bodies buried by civilians and disinterred for reburial in a military burial ground.

As the surveyor, I was usually in advance of my company, laying out the next burial ground. I always had my assistant, Vincent Goes Ahead, a Crow Indian, and a small squad with me to mark the individual graves. A burial platoon would follow in a few days.

I prepared a "log" book for each cemetery containing every angle, landmark, distance, and plot and sent it to the rear where draftsmen prepared a blueprint. They would frequently set up the drafting equipment in a church entry, to protect the drawings from the wind and rain. Churches were never locked, and Americans were welcome.

We had a medical staff that always checked each body and made dental charts, fingerprints, and dog tag identification. (Interestingly enough, sometimes our medical staff would be called away to villages to deliver babies.) When we were hastily burying large numbers, only the dog tag would be placed on the cross or the Star of David (for Jewish servicemen). Later the full name and company would be painted on the front of the marker. We always had truckloads of markers on hand or on order. The records were very detailed, and a chaplain would visit the cemetery frequently to provide services. Swiss representatives, being from a neutral country, checked both German and American units frequently to make certain that enemy dead were also given honorable burial. Later we would learn that the Germans performed well in this sensitive job also.

It was usually my duty to select a location for the cemetery and confiscate the land from the farmer, making certain the land had two access roads and a desirable slope. Civil Affairs would later pay the farmers five hundred dollars per acre for the land. That meant that nearly every plot had to be measured by square meters. Usually the land would belong to two or more farmers, and each must be paid equitably.

Early in my work, I found that a simple engineering job was needed, raising a flag pole. It was a nuisance job and wasn't getting done. It became a part of my job to have my translator bargain with a farmer to cut a tree suitable for a pole and drag it to the cemetery. Usually I would offer the farmer five cigarettes, and I'm sure they would gladly have continued dragging logs all day for that pay. Frequently they used oxen or cows to move the poles because most of their best horses had been confiscated by the Germans. I would then have a hole dug for the pole and a trench about ten feet long dug toward the hole. By backing a truck to the small end of the pole, attaching a pulley and rope to the top, lifting the end onto the truck and then slowly moving the truck in reverse, it took only three or four men to set the pole. With the American flag in place, we were officially a U.S. military cemetery. The idea for a simple way to raise these poles came from my experience setting hay poles.

When the plots were surveyed and pegged for each individual grave, it was necessary for a labor unit to dig the graves. American labor battalions were used within ten miles of the front. When the front lines were closer than ten miles, prisoners of war would be used to dig graves, and American soldiers became their guards. According to the Geneva Conventions, prisoners could be forced to work no more than ten hours per day. Therefore, if we had unusual needs, the American soldiers were required to go back to work. There was no limit to the hours a soldier could be on duty. A few times we had to go to a village and commandeer all the male population to get enough graves completed.

•

One of the worst periods of the war was the Battle of the Bulge. Thousands of Americans were bottled up by German forces for weeks on the border of France and Belgium. I was working from Headquarters at Fosses, Belgium, although we had winter quarters in Mettet, France, a village about seven miles west. We had lived in stables, machine sheds, and tents up to this point.

All soldiers in the European Theater were under stress during the Battle of the Bulge, and I don't want to fill this with gruesome tales, but I do want to talk about Christmas Day of 1944. There had been a lot of snow, and the Fosses cemetery was a mess. Christmas morning twenty-six trucks containing frozen, dead bodies came in from the "Bulge." Even cooks and clerks had to abandon their duties and help at the cemetery.

Then a radio call came into our headquarters requesting that I be sent to survey a bomb blast on the runway of the 5th Army Air Force. They were cut off from regular engineering service. Goes Ahead and I took a jeep and equipment and were there in an hour. This was a different type of surveying. I not only had to measure the width and length of the blast but also the depth and figure the number of cubic yards of fill required so the marooned planes could again take off.

That noon, Goes Ahead and I were invited to have Christmas dinner with the pilots. It was the first time in many months we were served with plates, knives, and forks instead of mess kits. The food was a real treat. Some folks were living far better than we were, but they had more dangerous jobs.

We got back to Headquarters about 4:00 P.M., and there was hot water for a shower. I cleaned up and gathered some little gifts for the Laine family [one of the French families with whom Chester had become friends] and went there for Christmas supper. Unfortunately, I told the company clerk where I would be.

Halfway through the meal there was a knock on the door and a message to return to Headquarters at once.

The Nijmegen Bridge across the Rhine had been damaged. There were many casualties, and there was immediate need for a burial ground in Molenhoek, Holland. These were mostly Canadian and British casualties, but their people couldn't get a graves unit across the Rhine.

Goes Ahead and I tried to round up a squad, but the only men available were six new replacements with no experience, fresh that day from the States. I always tried to use "green troops" in established cemeteries until they became psychologically prepared for handling mutilated bodies, but tonight was not the time for a training session.

We loaded the squad and equipment into a four-wheel-drive weapons carrier and headed northeast 168 kilometers (that's 105 miles). The cobblestone roads were covered with snow, and the fog was so dense I could scarcely see. All vehicles at that time had to travel with "Cat's Eyes" at night to prevent enemy observation of troop movement. (That means the headlights were painted leaving a half-inch crosswise streak for illumination.) Visibility was so poor that Goes Ahead had me stop. He took a big flashlight, climbed on the hood and pointed the light to the edge of the road. The pace was very slow and my squad was nervous, but we made it by 4:00 A.M. only to find the access bridge across a small river had been destroyed. The batteries in the flashlight were still fairly good so Goes Ahead and I started moving our equipment across the river by jumping from one chunk of ice to another. I got the squad across and kept them there, but Goes Ahead made three round trips to get vital equipment across. Our feet were soaked, but by daylight we were at work. There were frozen bodies ranked up like cordwood awaiting burial. One can understand why "Merry Christmas" had a hollow ring for me for years to come.

●

The next day, as we completed the first plot a labor platoon was moved in to start digging graves. As the fog cleared, we noticed there were people clinging to floating chunks of ice upstream. My inexperienced crew recovered twenty-three Dutch civilians and a few wounded Canadian soldiers. We got in contact with an emergency medical unit and they got them to safety. This brilliant sergeant who had pouted about having unseasoned troops found himself in command of a squad of "green troops" that was eligible for a Theater of Operations Commendation!

•

Goes Ahead and I noticed that our feet were becoming very tender so we thought perhaps we should report to a medical aid station. They confirmed that our feet had been frozen and gave us treatment. We were to report back every third day, but almost at once we were ordered to Son, Holland (pronounced Sawn), and were cut off from medical assistance for nine days. When we did report in, they immediately transferred us to an army hospital in Brussels for more intense treatment. The hospital was a deserted fire station with all windows and doors blasted out and covered with canvas, but they did have heat.

The doctor opened the purple blisters on our feet and treated us with a sulfa ointment, then replaced our combat boots with a transparent plastic sock and slippers. Then the doctors came up with a great idea. They would issue us new combat boots one half size too large so we could wear the plastic stockings filled with sulfa ointment plus some heavy socks and return to duty after two-and-a-half days.

•

Before a cemetery was closed and we moved on to the next location it was essential that religious burial rites be performed and validated for each plot. Normally, regimental chaplains came by each week to perform these services, but during the Battle of the Bulge they were frequently cut off from access. My translator and I would sometimes go to a village to get a priest or minister to perform the final service.

During this period of intense fighting, rapid movement, frozen feet, and exhaustion, I had an experience that would change my entire life in a negative way from a religious standpoint. We were hurrying to move on, and the Chaplain Services had been contacted. When the chaplain's driver pulled in he came to me to explain that the chaplain was too drunk to get out of the jeep and perform the service! At a time when "God's children" were frantically killing each other because of a maniac, Adolph Hitler, and we were all trying to function under stress, this was too much for my eyes. Why would a chaplain attempt to regain his strength from a whiskey bottle rather than from his faith?

This incident was at once followed by another disturbing episode. My interpreter and I hurried to a village to get a minister. I was shocked by his request, and even my French translator, who was only a boy of fourteen, was embarrassed as he translated. The minister's question was, "How many francs per grave will be donated to my ministry?" These American soldiers already had given their lives to liberate these people. Now there was to be a cash fee for each prayer?

My sister and I had been raised in a Christian environment, and religion was important to us. Now I was furious and confused. Ten percent of our company had been lost because of nervous disorders. Was I to become the next statistic?

When the war was over I started attending inter-faith chaplain services to get my thinking straightened out. I knew that I was wrong to base my feelings on the failings of two individuals, but I had lost my sincerity and enthusiasm to a serious degree. I still feel this was the most drastic repercussion of the war for me.

●

As the German forces crumbled, we crossed into Germany, and I was to establish my first cemetery on enemy soil. On May 7, 1945, word came down to us of the proclamation of V-E day (Victory in Europe). New orders started coming in. The first directive was that the cemeteries in Germany would be the first to be disinterred. No parents wanted sons to remain buried on enemy soil. It was decided which of the fifty-four burial grounds would be concentrated into six permanent cemeteries and turned over later to the Battle Monuments Commission. Again, our company would be ordered to start supervising the task.

Hermetically sealed caskets were shipped home for burial in family plots, but some Americans preferred that loved ones remain with army buddies.

I don't want you to think that your story has to be as dramatic as Chester's World War II stories. The other chapters of his book were interesting too, and I read every word. Both before and after the war he taught high school agriculture, and his life centered around his students, his farm, his farming community, and his family. His entire life has been full of "people stories," as all of our lives are, and he has recounted them throughout his book.

About three years ago, retired assistant postmaster Carl Nelson, called me from Whittier, California. (I mentioned him at the beginning of the previous chapter.) He said he had read my book and wanted to teach a class based on it in his church. He wanted to know how many people I thought he should have in a class. I told him I thought it would be best not to have more than fifteen. He put a notice about the class in his church bulletin and also in the local genealogical group's newsletter. A few weeks later he called me in a panic. Twenty-three people had signed up. What should he do with all of them? (Actually, I think he had already decided what to do before he called.) He decided to hold a morning class and an afternoon class. Calls began coming in for him to teach the class and to give speeches at retirement homes, at the YMCA, at genealogical groups, and in all sorts of places.

He asked where he could get the books in quantity, and I told him any bookstore could order them, or he could call my publisher, or he could order them direct from me. Everyone in the classes decided they would rather order them from me so they could be autographed.

Since they ordered them from me, I have been able to keep an account of how many Carl has ordered. He and I compared notes over the phone recently, and we think he has sold approximately 250 books. Think of how many lives he has touched and how many life stories have been written because of him!

Carl has sent me several stories from his classes and some that he has written about his own life. His experience in World War II was very different from Chester Graithwaite's, but he, too, wrote about something that has not been widely publicized—some personal stories about General Dwight D. Eisenhower from the point of view of some men who worked in close proximity to him.

First Carl tells us how he, a lowly corporal (later a sergeant), happened to be in such august company:

In October, 1943, after thirteen weary days of zigzagging across the Atlantic in a convoy, we finally dropped anchor in Liverpool. Our troopships belched forth GIs by the thousands—five thousand from our ship, to be exact. We were part of the buildup for the invasion of the European continent.

The outfit to which I was assigned was a Signal Corps company. I was a radio operator. I did not know it then, but we were scheduled to hit the beaches of Normandy one hour after the start of the invasion on D day.

We marched through Liverpool to the depot, where we were loaded onto tiny English trains and taken to the small village of Kingstanding, near Birmingham, there to await assignment to a larger Army unit.

The next morning, while we were lined up for roll call, I heard my name. "Corporal Nelson," bellowed the sergeant, in true sergeant fashion, "front and center." I "front and centered," wondering what breach of Army etiquette I had been guilty of. "Report to the gym," he commanded.

In the chill of that foggy English morning as I walked toward the gymnasium building, I wondered why I had been

singled out of that large group of men. I entered the temporary wooden structure that served as a gym and was met by a
well-pressed GI.

His uniform was immaculate, and his buttons glistened. I
must have presented a comic appearance, standing before him—
he, all spit and polish, and I, after thirteen days on the crowded
troopship in wrinkled uniform and combat shoes.

"I see by your record that you attended business college," he
said, "Do you take shorthand?"

"I could at one time." At that moment I wished a thousand
times over that I had continued to use shorthand after leaving
business school five years before. But I hadn't, and inwardly I
had a sinking feeling.

"Tomorrow morning at ten," continued the sergeant, "I'll
give you an examination."

He didn't tell me any more than that. That evening while the
rest of the boys were sitting around chewing the rag, I sat alone,
trying desperately to recall all of the outlines and brief forms
that I had not used for so long.

I reported back to the gym on schedule next morning. There
I was escorted into a small room, where I found the sergeant
sitting at a desk. On a table nearby was a typewriter. It looked
like a guillotine to me.

The sergeant claimed he dictated at about 90 words a minute.
To me, it seemed more like 190. When at last he finished and
told me to transcribe my notes, my hands were quivering like
aspen leaves in a spring breeze. Frankly, I didn't expect to pass
the examination. Too many years had whizzed by since I had
been in school. But Providence was kind to me. The sergeant
informed me that I had qualified, that I should go back to my
billet and await further instructions.

Qualified for what? That question was still uppermost in my
mind a few days later when my orders came and I said good-
bye to my buddies. That was the last time we were to meet
until after the invasion.

They assigned me to the office in London of General Devers, Commanding General, the man who preceded General Eisenhower. My knees must have sagged a little when I heard of my assignment. They put me on the night shift at first. I took dictation from an officer of summaries of all important wires that came through from the War Department during the night. I then had to transcribe them so the General could read them quickly the next morning. Many nights as I transcribed my notes, the building shook as bombs burst nearby. It wasn't easy to take dictation under those circumstances. Some of the words in my notebook looked a little zigzaggy.

Electrifying news came through shortly after I arrived at headquarters. General Eisenhower was to be placed in charge of the European Theater. There was an air of tenseness on the morning he arrived. All of us were curious to see him, and we also wondered if our jobs would be secure. We were soon put at ease. The General always had a way of putting people at ease in his presence.

Carl soon found this out on a very personal level:

One day when I was in a hurry and was descending the stairs in our London office two at a time with my head down, I suddenly sensed that someone was approaching. I stopped and looked up just in time to find myself nose to nose with General Eisenhower. Did Ike lose his temper? Did he stare me down in true military fashion? He did not. He simply smiled his famous smile and said, "Good morning, sergeant."

•

Once, I was ordered to Antwerp, Belgium, as the train secretary on General Eisenhower's private train. General Eisenhower didn't happen to be present on this trip. My bosses on the trip were five generals who had been sent over from Washington on an inspection tour. I shall never forget that trip—taking dictation on the train in Antwerp as V-2 rocket bombs fell on the nearby docks; then transcribing notes in the diner by candlelight, (using an old, tired portable machine), while the car swayed to and fro over the uneven rails.

During the trip and between rocket explosions, I was able to spend some time with the train commander, a captain. I asked him to tell me of a typical day when General Eisenhower was aboard.

The captain said, "Well, the first thing he does is say, 'Captain, let's get a cup of coffee and talk.' Then we sit down, and he quizzes me about the enlisted personnel comprising the train crew. You could never get him to talk about anything else but the enlisted personnel. 'Are they getting enough to eat?' the General always asks. 'What kind of food are they getting? At what intervals do they receive their meals? Are they getting proper rest between trips? Are you giving them time off now and then?' Like I said, I could never get him to talk about anything else."

●

After we moved to Frankfurt, one of the General's drivers came to me one day and told me about a PX he had seen on a side street. It had a sign that read, "Post Exchange, Generals Only." The driver told me, "If General Eisenhower knows that place exists, he'll blow his top." (Generals were not supposed to get special treatment in post exchanges. No doubt this one carried items that the regular ones didn't have.)

The driver said, "The next time I get a chance, I'm going to drive the General down that street so he can see that sign."

Three or four days later the driver had his opportunity. As he neared the sign, he drove quite slowly.

From the back seat came, "Sergeant. Stop the car!" The General leaned forward, pointing to the sign and asked, "What's the meaning of that sign?"

"Well, sir," said my friend, "I guess that's a PX for generals, only."

"Go in and ask the commanding officer to come out here."

In a few minutes the officer appeared with the driver. After asking about the sign, General Eisenhower said, "I want that sign to come down, and I want it to come down NOW! And I'll sit here until it's removed."

According to the driver, the sign came down post haste. "And," he said, "GIs practically came out of the woodwork and headed for the PX to get some of the goodies that up until then had been off limits."

•

You can certainly believe that General Eisenhower was a busy man. But he was a man with a heart. For example, when the U.S. troops moved to France, a number of soldiers left sad English girls behind. The girls would wait, often in vain, for letters from their American boyfriends or fiancés. Finally, in desperation, many of them wrote to General Eisenhower giving the young man's name and company. General Eisenhower always took these letters seriously. He answered each letter personally, advising the writer that he would contact the company commander and see what could be done about the problem. In other cases, he would actually pick up the telephone and call the young women in England in an effort to comfort and reassure them. Such a person was General Eisenhower.

One day, in a telephone conversation with Carl, I happened to mention that my niece and her husband were in Romania to adopt a little girl. Carl said, "Well, you know, both of our kids are adopted. In fact Ester (his wife) wrote a story about one of them for the class. I urged him to send it to me. I'm including part of it here because I like it very much and because I want to emphasize that it's just as important to write about day-to-day living as it is to write about dramatic episodes in your life and about famous people you have known.

Carl and I had been married for nine years when we finally adopted Linda, taking her directly from the hospital when she was just six days old.

A couple of years later we made application at the County Bureau of Adoption for another child. Our case worker, Miss Landon, seemed quite severe. Carl had a problem with her during one of her several interviews with us. One day she called Carl in and had a private talk with him. He came home really upset, because she had questioned him about what Quakers believe. She said it wasn't their policy to give a child to couples who were involved in "offbeat religions." Since I was a birthright Quaker (meaning I was born into a Quaker family) she felt Carl could be more objective about the church. Carl came away feeling we would never be given a child. Miss Landon seemed rather unsympathetic.

A few months later, when Linda was almost four years old, we got a call from Miss Landon. She had a boy for us. It had been a toss-up in the department as to whether the Nelsons or another family were to be offered the little boy. We learned later that they chose us for two reasons: 1) Both of our parents were living, so our children would have grandparents to love them, and 2) We were Quakers.

Later, Miss Landon told us she knew all about Quakers. Her college roommate was a Quaker. She was just testing Carl to see how badly he wanted another child.

We were told we could have our son if we chose. We must know first that he had spent the first three months of his life with his natural mother, during which time she was finally deciding it would be better for both if she put him up for adoption. Then, for the next four months, he had been in three foster homes. He was jaundiced and allergic to many foods, so would take special care. Would we be willing to take him? Yes we would!

A few days later we were to go into the Bureau with Linda, ready to bring home the newest member of our family. What a day! We three were in a state of high excitement—happy, yes, and scared a bit, too. When we arrived at the Bureau, Miss Landon took four-year-old Linda in first to see the baby. She asked Linda if she would like to have him for a brother, and Linda quickly agreed that she would, so Miss Landon and Linda came out with this sweet little seven-month-old boy and told us that Linda had chosen him for her brother. That was a wise bit of psychology on Miss Landon's part.

Here was our little boy, in a yellow corduroy suit and a little yellow corduroy hat that came around his face like an aviator's cap, and a complexion to match. He was yellow from the top of his cap to his tiny toes. The yellow outfit only accented the jaundice we had known he had.

Poor Miss Landon! She was so sorry that the foster family had chosen yellow in which to outfit him for his new family because it seemed to heighten the color of his skin, and another color could have played it down. Did we care? We certainly did not. We had our perfect little family—a girl and a boy—and who could ask for anything more.

Before we left, we were given a list of the things Bruce (we named him Bruce Earl) could not eat because of his allergies. No eggs—no milk—no, no, no. The list seemed endless, and his problem was that he would, or could hardly eat anything at all. Now I wonder how we dared think we could care for him properly, but somehow we felt that love and security could make a difference.

Feeding Bruce became the focus of my life for quite awhile. That little bundle simply refused to eat. I would spend an hour at each feeding time just to get him to eat a little bit. Dr. Barmore examined him, found he was suffering from malnutrition, and said that maybe it wasn't allergy—maybe it was trauma from being moved so often during his first seven months of life. Maybe with love and patience he would improve. So I started feeding him food he needed to be strong, even though they said he was "allergic." For weeks it still took an hour each time to feed him, but gradually it took less time, gradually he ate more food, and gradually he lost his jaundiced color and became a healthy little baby.

Much later, Miss Landon, so pleased with his progress, told us that his condition was such that if we hadn't taken him, they would have put him in a home for physically handicapped children. I shudder even today when I think about it. All that poor little baby needed was to know that he was loved and wanted. We had plenty of love to give him—all three of us—and we certainly wanted him.

Esther then goes on to tell how Bruce became a star of his Little League Baseball team and grew up to become a successful businessman with a wife and daughter. "Seeing Bruce now," she says, "and remembering the early days, I know I can't take all the credit for him. His transformation was actually a miracle, and our family witnessed it."

TWENTY-EIGHT

Research

You will note that when the woman in Chapter 26 wanted to find out about Amelia Bloomer, she went to the *library*, the place where she did all her research. I am devoting an entire chapter of this book to research and I hope everything in it will be helpful; however, absolutely the best piece of advice I can give you about research can be put into one sentence:

Ask your librarian!

If you are not accustomed to using a library for research you probably haven't realized what wonderful creatures librarians are. They are trained from the time they enter library science school to give service to the public. They are willing, even eager, to help you. In fact, friends of mine who are librarians sometimes express frustration that so few people actually know what services librarians have to offer.

Let me give you an example of how much information I gleaned from just one phone call to the reference department of the Kansas City Public Library. Remember the chapter on inventions in which the woman told about making ice cream at home "after there was an ice house in Lamoni"? When I read her story I began to wonder when ice cream was actually invented, so I called the library.

Here's what the librarian told me: no one knows for sure who invented ice cream. Marco Polo may have brought recipes from China for some water ices in 1295. In the 1600s Europeans used a combination of snow, ice, and saltpeter to freeze mixtures of cream, fruit, and spices.

English colonists probably brought recipes to America in the early 1700s. It was a luxury food which was always made at home until 1851 when Jacob Fussell established the first ice cream parlor, in Baltimore. In 1904, the ice cream cone was introduced at the World's Fair in St. Louis. Ice cream bars were introduced in 1920. Ice cream was not widely known outside of large cities until the second decade of the twentieth century, when ice began to become available to the average family. Not a bad collection of information for a five minute telephone call, is it?

If it is difficult for you to get out or if you have specific questions, librarians will nearly always be glad to help you by phone. I do want to point out, however, that you shouldn't ask a librarian to do too much for you that you can do for yourself. There aren't enough librarians to do all of your research for you. However, you will be amazed at the amount of help they can give you, and they are more than happy to show you how to locate information for yourself. It's fun to do as much of your research yourself as you possibly can because you stumble across all sorts of information that you didn't expect.

Completing the research for an autobiography nearly always takes less time and is less difficult than my students expect. The man who wrote the excellent historical setting for his personal part in D day did all of the necessary research in an afternoon. When I first suggested that he write an historical frame of reference for his story he objected strenuously. He said he couldn't possibly tackle anything like that, that he didn't remember ever having even been in the public library. He added that his wife had dragged him to the class with him protesting all of the way, that he hadn't read anything but the newspaper since he left high school, so he couldn't possibly do a lot of research.

I said, "You were caught up in the midst of D day. Wouldn't you be interested in knowing what your family and friends at home were reading about the invasion while you were there fighting?" He admitted that he would find that interesting.

D day was June 6, 1944, so I suggested that he go to the part of the library where microfilms of newspapers are kept and ask the librarian for the *Kansas City Star* and *The New York Times* for June 6, 7, 8, 9, and 10, 1944. I also suggested that he refer to the *Reader's Guide to Periodical Literature*, which is one of the writer's best tools. This series of reference books, one volume for each year, indexes all of the articles published in most (though not all) of the major magazines and tells when they were published and in which magazine. For example, in researching D day my student simply opened up the volume for 1944, looked up D day and found articles listed in *Time*, *Life*, *Newsweek*, *Saturday Evening Post*, *Colliers*, and many, many more publications.

I also suggested that he look up the topic in the *Encyclopedia Britannica*, *World Book Encyclopedia*, and in the card catalog. The card catalog, in case you aren't familiar with it, is a stack of drawers containing cards which list all of the books in the library. The books are listed on three different cards, each of which is filed alphabetically. One card is filed under the title of the book, one under the subject of the book, and the other is under the name of the author.

Since I first wrote this book nearly all large libraries, and many smaller ones, have acquired two computerized indexes, one for magazines and one for books. Don't let the word "computer" scare you as it did me for several months before I finally got up the courage to use these computers. It only takes a minute to learn how to use them. Easy-to-follow directions are always provided nearby, and if there's something you don't understand, ask the librarian to help you. He or she will be glad to show you what to do. (Don't worry, they expect people to ask questions and need assistance.) In case you are faint-hearted, the *Reader's Guide to Periodical Literature* and the card catalog are still available; but computerized lists are faster to use. Also, the computerized periodical list covers many more magazines than the *Reader's Guide* does.

After his trip to the library my student came to class in an absolutely jubilant mood. He had discovered a whole new world. His participation in the invasion of Normandy had been one of the most momentous events in his life and he discovered that he had never really realized the full scope of it until he began his library reading. For example, he had had only a hazy idea of the very extensive involvement of paratroopers in the operation.

He also told the class about another discovery he made. "You know you get pretty self-centered when you're in the middle of a battle," he said. "And we had been building up to the invasion for weeks and were pretty self-centered then, too. We just forgot that there was a war going on anywhere else. I found this article in *Time* telling about all of the fronts where battles were going on during the invasion of Normandy—six besides Normandy. God, the whole world was blowing up. I knew the piece of real estate where I was was blowing up but I had almost forgotten that they were fighting in Russia and Asia and Italy and in the Balkans and the South Pacific and the Adriatic, too. It was interesting to see what was happening in other parts of the world."

That's the kind of interesting surprises one encounters while doing research.

The sources I have mentioned above—newspaper microfilms, the Reader's Guide to Periodical Literature, encyclopedias, and the card catalog—are probably the most often used library tools.

There are many ways these sources can help you. For example, I was once writing an article for *Reader's Digest* about my memory of a very special Christmas. No one who had been involved in that particular Christmas celebration could remember for sure whether it was in 1952 or 1953, and for the purpose of my article I needed to be accurate. While I was trying to pinpoint the year, I happened to remember that when we were planning that Christmas everyone was talking about a ship which had broken in two in the North Atlantic. Great excitement surrounded the breaking up of the *Flying Enterprise*, and I was sure all of the national magazines had carried stories about the ship. I went to the library, checked the *Reader's Guide to Periodical Literature* for 1952 and 1953, and there in 1952 was a whole list of articles about the *Flying Enterprise*. My year was 1952.

The woman who wrote the eyewitness account of the San Francisco earthquake wanted to add some statistical information to her story to help her readers understand the actual extent of the quake's damage. She looked in the *World Book Encyclopedia* under San Francisco and in a few minutes found everything she wanted to know.

As you write your story, questions about dates, places, occasions, and more, will arise. Ask yourself whether there is some way newspapers or magazines of the day can help augment your memory or add interest to your story. Or perhaps some factual information from a book or an encyclopedia will help.

Valuable as the four tools mentioned above are, they represent only a fraction of the research sources available in the library. Libraries are an almost bottomless well of indexes, special interest encyclopedias, almanacs, and more.

You will gradually become familiar with many of these sources as you use the library. However, only librarians have the specialized knowledge to know all of the institution's resources, and they expect to be asked for their help.

Never be afraid that your question is silly or will seem silly to a librarian. A couple of years ago I was editing an article for the *Overland Journal*; the author mentioned the name of a young army captain who was killed in an encounter with some Indians in the 1850s. Unfortunately he only gave me the captain's last name. I called the author to ask him to supply the first name but found he was out of town. I felt it would be bad form to publish the article with only the captain's last name, so I called the reference room at the library. As many times as librarians have been able to give me the most obscure bits of information, this seemed to me to be an impossible request. I didn't know the man's unit, and it wasn't even a major Indian battle. It was just a skirmish between a few soldiers and a few

Indians out in the middle of nowhere. When the librarian came on the line I asked the question somewhat apologetically.

"Just a moment, I'll see," she said in her cheery voice, and in a couple of minutes she was back with the captain's first name.

After thanking her I said, "Well I certainly thought I'd stump you with that question; I almost didn't call."

She answered, "Oh, always call. Once in awhile we get a question we can't answer but not very often, and it would be a shame for you to miss getting the information just because you didn't call. Chances are we'll have it someplace, although sometimes it takes a little longer for us to find it than other times."

In my opinion all librarians should be canonized!

Even if your library doesn't have the information you need, your librarian may be able to help you get it. If you want a specific book and your library doesn't have it, there is a good chance your librarian can get it for you on an interlibrary loan. In many instances your librarian can also obtain photocopies of magazine and newspaper articles from other libraries.

There are many other sources of information besides your local library. Every state has an historical society, as does nearly every town and county. The state societies are usually well staffed with professionals who can answer questions for you. County, town, and specialized societies sometimes have paid staffs too, but often they are staffed only by volunteers. This may mean there won't be anyone to answer your inquiry, but if you have a specific question which you think a certain society might be able to answer, it won't take much time or money to write them a letter. You might get very good results.

I have a friend, Fred Lee, who is a volunteer archivist for Kansas City's Westport Historical Society. Frequently when we are talking he will say something like, "I got the most interesting letter today. A woman whose great grandfather had a blacksmith shop here around 1880 wanted to know if we had any information about him." Far from feeling that the writer is imposing, Fred enjoys answering questions submitted to him. Many small historical societies with only volunteer staffs are diligent about collecting information and are delighted when someone needs the materials they have collected so lovingly. Your librarian can help you locate the names and addresses of many of these historical societies.

When you write an historical society you should send a stamped, self-addressed envelope. All of them, whether large or small, whether staffed by volunteers or professionals, are short of funds. They ask no pay, or very little pay, for the help they give you, but it shouldn't cost them anything either.

When it comes to researching your ancestors, I advise you not to go any farther back than your grandparents or great grandparents for the purpose of your autobiography. If you try to reach beyond your great grandparents you may find yourself bogged down in your research and distracted from writing your autobiography. Tracing one's genealogy is a fascinating game, but it is so time consuming that I advise you to postpone any extensive ancestor sleuthing until after you have finished your autobiography. To give you an idea of just how overwhelming genealogical research can be—if you go back ten generations on both sides of your family you have 1,024 ancestors.

The first and most important way to begin researching your ancestors is among your living relatives, the older they are, the better. When you are talking with relatives it is a good idea to get the names of their relatives too. Sometimes recollections which have been forgotten by one branch of the family are handed down by another. Be sure to get complete names of ancestors, both maiden names and married names, given names and nicknames. My nephew was once looking for some information about an ancestor of ours whose name was Alpheus Cutler. After many hours of fruitless searching he discovered that Alpheus Cutler's middle name was John and that many of the financial records concerning him were in the name of John rather than Alpheus. None of us had ever known that John was his middle name. So, you see, it pays to get every scrap of information you can when you are researching your ancestors.

Visit as many relatives as possible and take notes or tape record your conversations. If there are relatives whom you wish to question but whom you can't visit, write them. It's a good idea to avoid asking just general questions and to be as specific as possible. One of my students made up a questionnaire with blanks to be filled in, had it photocopied, and sent it to a lot of relatives. This made answering her questions easy, and she got an excellent response. Here, too, you should enclose a stamped, self-addressed envelope when you ask for information to be mailed to you.

Another good source of information about ancestors is cemeteries. In many cemeteries, particularly old ones, the deceased's parents' names are on the tombstones; that is, "here lies so-and-so, son of so-and-so." Sometimes you can add another whole generation to your list just by reading one headstone.

The following helpful booklets have been compiled by the National Office of Vital Statistics, Public Health Service, United States Department of Health and Human Services:

Where to Write for Birth and Death Records
(Public Health Publication No. 630A, 15c)

Where to Write for Marriage Records
(Public Health Publications No. 630B, 10c)

Where to Write for Divorce Records
(Public Health Publication No. 630C, 10c)

These three pamphlets cover all states and territories and are available from:

Superintendent of Documents
United States Government Printing Office
Washington, D.C. 20402

A wealth of information is also available through the National Archives. Suppose, for example, that you know your father fought in World War I, and you want to know which company he was in, when he was discharged, or where he fought. This information is available from:

Military Service Records (NNCC)
National Archives (GSA)
Washington, D.C. 20408

I, of course, can't hope to tell you where to look for every bit of information you might need, but the suggestions in this chapter will get you started. The exciting thing about research is that one thing leads to another, one source suggests another. It's like playing detective. I think you will find it a very exciting part of writing your autobiography.

Now that we are in the computer age, I suppose I would be remiss if I didn't mention the internet as a research tool. Eight years ago, when home computers were just becoming widely available and affordable, I had an experience that opened up a whole new world to me. A writer in California who sent me an article for publication in the *Overland Journal* included some quotes from two 1841 newspapers published in small Missouri towns. Both papers had been out of print for more than a century. One of the towns is now so small, it isn't even shown on the map, and the other one no longer exists. I asked, "How on earth did you get those obscure quotes? Have you been to Missouri doing some research?"

"No," he answered casually. "I got them from the Library of Congress with my computer." I had heard that in some wonderfully mysterious way it was possible to do research on a computer, but here was someone who had actually *done* it! I was still in the stage where I thought computers were just heavenly because I didn't have to make ugly eraser marks on my paper and could make as many copies as I wanted without using carbon paper. Now, of course, millions of people are using the internet for research. It isn't difficult once you learn how. I won't try to tell you how in a few short sentences, but I can say that nearly all junior colleges have courses on how to turn a computer into a research tool. Also, I found the book *The Internet Research Guide*, by Timothy K. Maloy, helpful and I recommend it for anyone who knows absolutely nothing about researching on the Internet.

The internet address for the Library of Congress is: http://www.loc.gov. But this isn't the only source of information. Here again your librarian may be able to help you. Most libraries have on-line connections with many research libraries and large metropolitan libraries. They can give you the internet addresses of the ones they use and perhaps some they don't.

Wonderful as the Internet is for research, don't feel left out if you aren't on-line (or even if you don't have a computer). Remember, millions upon millions of books were researched and written before the Internet or computers ever came into existence.

Revising and
Pulling It
All Together

*H*ave you finished writing all of your assignments? Have you done the research that is necessary to fill in any blanks you may have? If so, you are ready to begin revising.

You are in a wonderful position to make revisions in your stories because you have been writing them over a period of weeks or months so what you have written is cold. In other words, you have been away from your stories for long enough so that it will be almost as if you are reading them for the first time. This will make it possible for you to spot necessary changes much more readily than if you were reading stories you had just finished writing.

When you begin revising, ask yourself the following questions:

1. **Is each story as clear and as well organized as you can possibly make it?**

   One woman wrote an interesting story about a clever thing her father did to help the people of his town during a terrible drought. Then she described the drought—hot sun; people who went out of doors having to cover their faces to keep from strangling on the dry dirt and sand that blew almost constantly for weeks; dry wells; dying cattle; and more. It was a vivid picture of the drought. However, since the description of the drought didn't come until after the story about her father we were wondering all of the time we were reading about him why he behaved as he did. We clarified the story by reversing its order, putting the description of the drought first. Thus we set the stage for the reader to understand her father's actions.

Check each story. Do you have the facts, the descriptions, and so on, in the right order for clarity?

2. **Is each sentence as clear as you can make it?**

Ask yourself whether some of the sentences are too long and complex. Perhaps some of the longer sentences would work better as two or three short sentences.

3. **Are there some words which you have used over and over again to the point where they begin to detract from your story?**

A writing teacher once said of one of my articles, "Lois, I think you have a salable article here except that you have about twenty "littles" and at least eighteen of them have to go." When she read the article aloud to the class I realized that I had written about a little girl, her little hands, her little shoes, her little dress, her little voice, and more.

Look for words which you have overworked. Maybe you can cut some of them entirely or maybe you can substitute another word. I recommend that you get a *Roget's Thesaurus of the English Language* if you don't already have one. This book gives many alternatives for thousands of words and will help you find another word to use instead of the one you are overworking. It will also help you find exactly the right word for what you want to say. (Mark Twain once said that the difference between using the right word and using almost the right word is the difference between a bolt of lightning and a lightning bug.)

This thesaurus is available in paperback. Get the one that is alphabetized instead of the original one, which lists words in categories. It's much easier to use. Just ask the clerk in the bookstore for an alphabetical *Roget's Thesaurus*. If it doesn't say "alphabetical" on the cover, try another store because an alphabetized edition definitely is available.

4. **Do your stories need cutting?**

Unless you hope to publish some of your stories you won't *need* to read the chapter called "Publishing Your Stories" unless you *want* to. However, at the end of that chapter there are three suggestions, which I have numbered. I recommend you read number three. It is about cutting and applies to all writing, whether or not it is intended for publication.

5. **Have you used narrative where you could have used dialogue?**

Look for places where you can make your story more interesting by repeating actual conversations rather than just summarizing them.

6. **Have you used a lot of clichés, that is, trite phrases?**

Trite phrases sprinkled throughout your manuscript will lessen its impact. Avoid saying something is "as good as gold," someone is "as pretty as a picture," or "they were loud in their praises." These are all overworked, hackneyed phrases which slip out naturally in conversation but when written down "stand out like a sore thumb" and diminish your work.

7. **Have you clearly identified every relative you mention?**

You don't want someone a couple of generations from now to be reading your story and come across a mention of Uncle George and have to wonder whether he was their great uncle or their great, great uncle. Nor should they have to wonder whether he is from your father's or mother's side of the family. Remember the trouble my sisters and I had trying to figure out whether the woman the Indians put in the tree was our great grandmother or our great great grandmother.

Of course, you have to fully identify each relative only once, preferably the first time you mention him or her. After that just the name will suffice.

8. **Have you told enough about the characters in your stories for your readers to be able to see and understand them?**

The writer of the story about the winter picnic did a very good job of describing her aunt. By calling her a city dweller, whose idea of roughing it was putting the thermostat down to 72, and by saying that her aunt swore she didn't go outdoors until she was 30, she gave us a clear picture of a fairly sophisticated, rather funny woman. In the story about Zachary, the little brother who died, the description of the child's hair, "soft, black, and curly like lamb's wool," helps create an endearing picture of him.

Check your manuscript against our ground rules, particularly rules three, four, and nine: be honest; don't let your story be just a sterile recital of events; and describe the scene in which the event took place. Remember how the story about the ice cream was enhanced by the description of the mother and three little daughters being outdoors looking at a rainbow when the father came walking through the orchard? The writer could have left all of that information out and just talked about the ice cream, but by including it she created a beautiful little scene and made her story come to life.

Now, about pulling it all together. The order in which you place your stories is completely up to you. Maybe you will want to leave them in the notebook just as they are and let each story stand alone. That would be perfectly appropriate.

However, if you want to make them into one continuous narrative they will have to be organized. Here is where reading some published autobiographies will help. Read one or two with organization in mind. Notice as you read them whether they started with the subject's birth or with the present and then return to his birth.

One of our assignments in class is "Your Plans for the Future." For this assignment, one woman wrote that she had taken care of sick people all of her life; first her parents, then her children, then her invalid husband. Now her parents and husband are dead and her children are on their own and she is going to do what she has wanted to do for years—write. She used this story of her plans for the future as the first chapter of her book. It sounds a little grim for a beginning, but it isn't. There is no bitterness in her story, no self-pity, and a great deal of love. The impression is of one who has always taken life as it comes and who is continuing to do so. After this chapter she goes to her birth and then continues chronologically.

Go back and reread the story about the woman who was confined to a wheelchair and started a prayer chain. She starts her book with a day in her life when several things have happened to make her realize how many people the prayer chain is helping. Then she tells how she happened to start the prayer chain, about her automobile accident, her triumph over her self-pity, and more. From then on her story is chronological, beginning with her birth. Her plans for the future come at the end of her book.

Perhaps you have an especially interesting story about one of your great grandparents which would make a good opening for your book. You could then move through information about your grandparents and your parents to your own birth.

The woman who wrote the story about being born in New Mexico before it was a state used that story as a beginning for her book. One student, who was born in 1898, was born prematurely and her birth story describes the primitive methods used by her parents and a country doctor to keep her alive. This story made a good beginning for her book.

If you are very young and have more of your life ahead of you than behind you, you may want to keep writing on a day-to-day or week-to-week basis, like a journal, for a while, leaving the arrangement of your book for a much later date.

If you decide to put your story into one continuous narrative you will need to write some bridges so that one story will lead smoothly into another. Some of these bridges will be only a sentence or two. Sometimes they may be several paragraphs. You may even think of another incident which will bridge the gap between one story and another.

In the chapter on toys I wrote a bridge which I used to tie a story from the distant past to a story from the recent past. You might find rereading this bridge helpful in writing your own bridges between incidents.

There is no right or wrong way to put your story together. If you have written all or most of the assignments you have created a wonderful legacy for your children and their children. Nothing you can do will ruin that. You may be able to enhance your stories by the way you arrange and connect them, but you can't diminish them, so move ahead with confidence.

Publishing Your Stories

I promised to give you some suggestions about shaping one or more of the incidents in your life into an article suitable for publication. If you aren't interested in publishing, perhaps you will want to skip this chapter, or you may read it just as a matter of interest to get some idea of how an article goes together.

The first thing you must do, of course, is decide which incidents in your life are suitable for publication. Not all incidents, no matter how interesting, form the basis for a salable article. Here are some tests to apply to your article ideas.

- Does the incident prove something?

- Will it help the reader in some way?

- Will it give the reader some important or at least some very interesting information?

Let's consider some of the stories in this book. The story about the little boy who made up his own language is an example of a very interesting story which probably would not make a salable article.

True, it is a fascinating and unusual incident, but that's just its problem. It may be too unusual. If thousands of American children were being brought up in nurseries, a story could make the point that there may be some drawbacks to excluding children from the family circle. Or if there were thousands of households in which five languages were spoken, one might make a case for everyone speaking the same language to children in the family.

I am not saying that no one in the world could make a salable article out of this incident, but I personally can't think of any possibilities for it. While unusual incidents and unusual variations on ordinary incidents are the stuff of which articles are made, an incident should not be so unusual that the reader can't relate to it.

On the other hand, the story by the young woman who systematically put pleasant thoughts instead of unpleasant thoughts into her head might be shaped into a very salable article. Which of us doesn't need to learn that lesson? And which of us couldn't profit from reading about the woman who, after being crippled in an automobile accident, overcame her destructive self-pity and now lives a happy and productive life? The Jewish woman who told how she and her husband finally accepted their Gentile son-in-law might write a story emphasizing the fact that love can overcome prejudice.

The lady who survived the San Francisco earthquake probably couldn't sell her story to a magazine, but she might sell it to her local newspaper, which would be very likely to publish it on the anniversary of the big quake. I had a student who wrote a delightful story about a day which he spent at the circus when he was seven years old. I told him to wait until about six weeks before the circus came to town and to send it to his local newspaper with a note asking whether the editor might be interested in publishing it in connection with the arrival of the circus. The editor bought it.

After selecting the incident about which you want to write, the next thing to decide is which editor or editors might want to buy your story. The best way to do this is to go to the library and study the current issue of *Writer's Market*. You will find it at the reference desk of any large library, or any book store can order it for you if they don't already have it. This book lists literally thousands of places for writers to sell their work. Each publication is listed under the appropriate heading; that is, women's magazines, religious magazines, and so forth. Under the name of the publication is a description of what kind of material the editor wants, how long an article should be, and so forth.

But don't consider that just studying *Writer's Market* is enough. After you decide on several possible markets for your article, you must study the publications carefully, even if they are ones you read regularly. You have probably been just reading them up until now—not studying them. Let me give you an example of the difference.

I know an elderly woman whose income is far below the poverty level. She is blind and her health is so bad that she almost never leaves her home. Sounds pretty grim, doesn't it? But this woman is a thoroughly happy person. She believes God expects her to be useful to the very end of her life and she acts accordingly. Nearly all of her waking hours are spent doing something for others. She has even been credited with saving two lives. I intend to write an article about her and I am almost certain that some publication will buy it.

First, I thought I'd trying marketing it to a publication called *Guideposts*. According to *Writer's Market* it is an inspirational magazine which tells how men and women "overcame obstacles, rose above failures, met sorrow, learned to master themselves, and became more effective people through the direct application of the religious principles by which they live." Sounds exactly right for my lady, doesn't it?

I have read many issues of *Guideposts* and even sold the editor an article once. I thought I knew exactly what was suitable for the magazine. Fortunately, before going my cocksure way I picked up a copy of *Guideposts* at a friend's house and leafed through it. I mentioned that my subscription had expired and that I must renew it. She went into her study and came back with a stack of *Guideposts*. "Here," she said, "I've finished with these. You might as well take them."

The next day I decided to read a few articles in the magazine before writing my own article. Well, studying those magazines saved me the disappointment of receiving a rejection slip. I discovered that my article wouldn't have been right for *Guideposts* at all. What they use is first person articles in which people themselves write about how they "overcame obstacles, rose above failure, met sorrow, learned to master themselves, and became more effective people" through the direct application of religious principles. My woman would have had to write the article herself in order for *Guideposts* to buy it. They wouldn't want the article I had planned. However, there was a way I could write the article for *Guideposts*. I could write an "as told to" article; that is, write it in the first-person voice of the woman, but admit that I had done the actual writing. You see, I needed to study that magazine.

After you have decided on the theme of your article, and possible markets for it, it is time to think about its framework.

Max Gunther, a highly successful freelance writer, once compared the framework of a good magazine article to the construction of a building. Any good building, whether it is a log cabin or a skyscraper, is built on the same principle. Each building, regardless of its size and architectural style, has its own structural logic. Its parts are not in random order. This particular beam rests on that particular wall. This timber accepts the stress of that wall. The architect knows all of this, but the person living or working in the building doesn't have to worry about it. So it should be with an article. The writer is aware of its framework, but the reader enjoys reading it, completely unaware of its technical construction.

Let's analyze my story "Breakfast on the Beach," not because I think it is an example of superlative writing, nor do I even think it is the best thing I have ever written. However, it is based on an incident in my own life, just as your story will be based on an incident in your life. An editor liked it well enough to buy it and readers liked it well enough to write me about it. Also, it is a simple, straight-forward story with a framework which is easy to analyze. Its framework consists of four parts:

1. the lead

2. the transition

3. the body

4. the conclusion

Some articles which are more complicated will have one or two more parts—some will have a section which is a restatement of their theme, for example. A controversial article will undoubtedly have a section which anticipates opposition. However, all articles have at least the four parts listed above. Some writers call them by different names but the parts are the same. There are, of course, occasional off-beat articles which have a completely different framework or no apparent framework at all. These articles are rare, however, and are usually written by experienced writers who know the rules so well that they consciously depart from them.

The first paragraph of "Breakfast on the Beach" constitutes its entire lead. (Sometimes a lead might run two or three paragraphs, never more.) Let's reread the paragraph:

1. If I hadn't been in very great need about a year ago, I might never have grasped the full significance of what has become one of my favorite Biblical passages. More important, I might never have known so surely the depth of God's concern for our practical, everyday needs.

In the lead I tell the reader that I am going to share with him a personal experience which will prove to him that God is concerned about our everyday needs. Although it is not specifically stated, it is implied that if the reader has a need he, too, can hope to receive help from God.

Having caught the reader's interest (I hope) and having told him what I am going to tell him, I move on to paragraphs two and three, which form the transition. In this section I give the reader the background information he needs in order to understand the story. I describe a writing assignment I have received and explain why it might present some difficulties for me. The transition bridges the way for the reader to move easily and with understanding from the lead to the body.

2. An amusement park in South Missouri, which might be called a "Disneyland of the Ozarks," had hired me to do a writing assignment. The park is a complete 1880 village with an atmosphere of quiet, nostalgic charm combined with Ozark hillbilly hijinks. Throughout the day, at various points in the park, actors and actresses perform short plays, five to seven minutes in length. My assignment was to rewrite, sharpen, and improve twelve of the scripts already in use and to write four completely new ones.

3. It was a particularly difficult kind of writing. Each of these very short plays had to have a complete plot. They had to be based on hillbilly humor, which was completely new to me. They had to have both dialogue and vaudeville-type sight gags, and they had to be funny enough to cause people to stand in the blazing Ozark sun to watch them.

In paragraph four I begin the body of the article. I talk about working on the writing assignment and describe how I began getting into trouble. Paragraph five heightens the problem. Paragraph six introduces a possible solution, and I take action.

4. I tackled the rewrites with enthusiasm. Before long, my typewriter was spelling "get" with an "i" instead of an "e," dropping its g's and saying "Ah" instead of "I," and I was having lots of

fun. But as I neared the end of the rewrite part of the assignment, a feeling of uneasiness began to steal over me. Soon I would have to start on the original scripts, and I didn't know what I was going to write about. In spite of the fact that I had been studying comedy writing and Ozark lore for weeks, I didn't have a single idea.

5. By the time I typed the final rewrite script, I was in a state of panic. The next day I would have to start writing the new scripts, and my deadline was just two weeks away. Still no ideas! I lay awake most of that night worrying and searching every corner of my brain for just the beginnings of a plot.

6. While I was eating breakfast the next morning, I remembered once hearing a minister say that when one is facing a dilemma it is a good idea to open the Bible at random, and sometimes the book will automatically open to a page that will provide an answer to the dilemma. At the time I thought the minister was talking nonsense. Still, I was completely sunk and anything seemed worth a try. Without really expecting to find anything helpful, I picked up the Bible. I opened it to one page—nothing that helped. I opened it a second time—still nothing. I opened it a third time—this time to the twenty-first chapter of John.

Paragraphs seven, eight, nine, ten, eleven, and twelve give me the basis for having faith that God will help me solve my problem. Note that this part of the body starts slowly in paragraph seven and then accelerates. It builds until I receive an important insight at the end of paragraph eleven.

7. The chapter tells of Jesus appearing on the beach at the Sea of Tiberias after his resurrection. He called to His disciples who

were fishing in a boat offshore, and asked if they were catching anything. The disciples called back that they were not. Jesus answered, "Shoot the net to starboard and you will make a catch."

8. The disciples followed His instruction, and within seconds their net was so full of fish they could scarcely haul it aboard. Immediately, they realized that the man on the beach must be Jesus and they rushed to greet Him.

9. When they arrived on the beach, Jesus had a fire going and was roasting fish and bread over a charcoal fire. "Come and have breakfast," He called.

10. As I finished reading the passage, it was as if someone had turned on a light in my head. I had one of those moments of illumination when the Spirit teaches us more in seconds than we could learn in a lifetime of living. I knew that although there had been other times when Jesus had provided food in more spectacular ways—multiplying a little basket of loaves and fishes to feed the multitude, turning water into wine—this particular story of Jesus the Provider was unique.

11. The earlier stories of Jesus miraculously providing food and drink had occurred before His resurrection, when He was still in His human state. This incident occurred after His resurrection, when He no longer had physical needs Himself. It demonstrated to me that His translation from the physical state did not lift Him above an interest in the physical needs of His friends. He had only a few short days on earth before He was to make His final departure. Yet part of that precious time He spent helping His disciples improve their financial condition by telling them where to fish; and part of the time He spent caring for their physical needs by preparing breakfast for them.

12. The story told me that God is vitally interested in our everyday problems. (After all, what is more mundane than preparing break-

fast?) I knew He would help me write my plays. Writing them was my job, part of my means of earning a living.

In paragraphs thirteen and fourteen I describe how I used my new insight and paragraphs fifteen and sixteen (the last two paragraphs of the body) tell how God answered my prayer.

13. I closed my eyes and said, "Father, you know I have this job to do and You know I need Your help. I'm sure You didn't give me the job so I could fail at it, so please help me."

14. I decided that having offered this prayer I would stop worrying and assume that my answer was on its way. I began washing the breakfast dishes, occupying my thoughts with what I was going to fix for dinner that night.

15. Suddenly, there came rushing into my head, crowding out all thought of dinner menus, the entire script for a play, with all the characters and dialogue intact. When this play was performed, it ran about seven minutes, so it seems logical that it should have taken at least that long for its dialogue to run through my mind. It didn't, though; I had it all in a second or two.

16. I almost ran to my typewriter. I sat down and wrote the entire script without stopping. I retyped it once the next day, changing only a word or a punctuation mark here and there, and it was finished. God had done my work for me. Not only that, He had done it superbly. The script had exactly the zany humor and hill-billy flavor it needed but it also had a grace and charm that I would never have dreamed possible in that kind of a script.

Paragraphs seventeen and eighteen form the conclusion:

17. Of course, I still had three plays to go and still no ideas, but I knew the ideas would come. My panic was gone, leaving my mind free for an inflow of ideas. I wrote those three scripts in much the same way I would write anything else, with ideas coming in bits and pieces, with lots of rewriting, rearranging, and polishing, but I was always confident that God was helping me. I met my deadline and the people at the park were delighted with the plays.

18. I believe that God gives us the particular soul adventure we need at each stage of our development. He taught me through that incident that He is willing, even eager, to help us meet the most practical needs of our everyday lives if we will ask for His help and have faith that He will give it.

Note that paragraphs seventeen and eighteen bring the article full circle from the lead by restating the theme. In other words, if you were to read only the first and last paragraphs of the article, you would still know what the article is about. There is an old journalism saying that when you write an article the first thing you do is tell them what you are going to tell them. Then you tell them. Then you tell them what you told them.

This doesn't mean you have to hit the reader over the head with a sledgehammer when stating your theme. Not all articles present their themes as explicitly in the lead and conclusion as I did in "Breakfast on the Beach." Sometimes I don't myself. There are many variations to the full circle, but in general it is an integral part of every well-written article.

I first heard about the full circle at a writer's conference at the University of Indiana. The moment I got home I grabbed a stack of magazines and read the first three and the last three paragraphs of every article in every magazine to see whether it was true. It is!

If you are serious about writing for publication I suggest that you, too, sit down and analyze a dozen or so articles. Look not only for the full circle aspect of their construction but study their entire framework. You'll be amazed at how much you will have learned by the time you finish.

Sometimes students, particularly my younger students, ask whether all of this tight structure doesn't stifle creativity. The answer is definitely not! It frees you to be more creative. It doesn't matter how many good ideas you have if you go wading around in a confused morass trying to figure out what to do with them.

Here are some additional suggestions about writing for publication:

1. **Don't try to put everything you know into one article.** Include only the material which that particular article demands. Once a writer suggested that I take a paragraph out of an article before I submitted it to an editor. I argued that I loved that paragraph. He, however, insisted that it didn't belong in the article. (Incidentally, I knew in my heart that he was right, but I couldn't stand to part with the paragraph.) My friend said, "I'll tell you what you do. You copy that paragraph on a white card and file it, then cut it out of the article. That way, you can get it out and read it whenever you want to but you won't bother your readers with it." Great advice!

2. **Face the fact that the chances of getting your story right the first time are almost nil.** I have read about writers who write their articles once, send them off the day they are finished, and sell them immediately. I have no doubt that somewhere in the world there are a few such fortunate souls. I certainly am not one of them, nor have I ever met one personally.

I don't believe I have ever considered an article finished in less than three drafts, four or five are more likely. I have occasionally even written as many as ten drafts for one article. This sounds grueling, and sometimes it is. Often, though, I find rewriting extremely rewarding. With each draft I get some new ideas, thus each rewrite becomes more creatively rewarding. It's wonderfully satisfying when you are typing along on a third or fourth draft wishing you didn't have to slog through the whole thing one more time to suddenly, out of nowhere, have a marvelous new idea about the story come swirling into your consciousness.

Don't do your second draft the minute you finish your first draft. Let it cool for a couple of days. You will spot more mistakes that way and you will also have more time to generate new ideas, which will enrich your next draft.

3. **Be careful about using too many words.** This, one of the best writing lessons I ever had, was from the editor of *U.S. Lady*, a magazine for the wives of American servicemen. She bought the first article I ever sold. Before buying it, however, she sent it back to me with a note saying I would have to cut it in half. Cut it in half? Impossible!

I pouted for a few days and then decided that I desperately wanted to sell that article so I set about following her instructions. Which parts should go? It seemed nothing could be spared. I finally started cutting a word here and a sentence there.

As I worked on the article I made a wonderful discovery. Cutting a word here and a sentence there was exactly what the article needed. I managed to get rid of half of the article without removing one single important point. I discovered that I had written a very loose, wordy, overblown article. When I cut it in half I had a tight, fairly well written piece.

The lesson that editor taught me made it possible for me to stop being an aspiring writer who was trying unsuccessfully to sell and become a professional writer who sold rather steadily. I shall always be grateful to her. (I hasten to add that you shouldn't depend on an editor to tell you how to salvage an article. *U.S. Lady's* rates weren't high. Consequently, the editor probably needed articles badly. Also, the subject of my article was particularly timely. If it hadn't been for these two facts, she probably would have returned my sloppy story with a routine rejection slip after reading two or three paragraphs. I was just lucky.)

If you haven't written a lot, you probably have a tendency to be too "wordy." After years of writing I still have that problem. What saves me is that I know I have it so I diligently look for places to cut in each draft of an article.

One good way of cutting is to make one word do the work of two or three whenever possible. For example, in this chapter I wrote the following sentence in my first draft:

"If thousands of children in America were being brought up in nurseries, a story could be written about the fact that there may be some drawbacks to not making the child part of the family circle."

Quite an unwieldy mouthful, isn't it? Here is the way it read after I got rid of the superfluous words:

"If thousands of American children were being brought up in nurseries, a story could make the point that there may be drawbacks to excluding children from the family circle."

I cut six words from a thirty-six-word sentence (one-sixth of the sentence) without changing the meaning, and I wound up with a less cumbersome sentence.

One of my besetting sins is saying the same thing twice. I say it in a different way each time, of course, but nevertheless I really need to say most things only once. This is something you might watch out for, too.

I have a rule which I impose on myself. Once I think I have done all I can do to a story I tell myself that I must cut another 10 percent of the words. Sometimes I have done my work well enough that I can't find that many words to cut, but I nearly always find a few words that can go—sometimes even 10 percent. Invariably these final cuts tighten and improve the story. I recommend this rule to you.

There are many wonderful, helpful books for people who want to teach themselves to write. I wish someone had told me about them when I began trying to learn. I had to stumble onto them all by myself over a period of years. There are many excellent books on how to write both fiction and nonfiction. Ask your librarian or bookseller to recommend some.

Below is a monthly magazine that is crammed with helpful articles for writers:

Writer's Digest
9933 Alliance Road
Cincinnati, Ohio 45242

This magazine is available at many libraries. It includes advertisements for many books on writing. Additionally, there are many helpful books on writing in most public libraries.

I can't teach you how to write a salable article in one chapter of one book. In fact, there is a consensus among writers that no one can teach another person to write, that each person must teach himself to write. A teacher can, however, show a beginning writer some shortcuts and give a few helpful hints. That is what I have tried to do in this chapter. I have given you enough hints to start you on the road to teaching yourself to write a salable article and to selling it if this is what you really want.

I leave you with two pieces of good news and a piece of bad news. First, a piece of good news is that I am absolutely positive that if you can write it you can sell it. The bad news is that writing for publication is very hard work. A final piece of good news: it's worth it! Good luck if you decide to try.

THIRTY-ONE

Your Special Privilege

I hope that by the time you reach this last chapter of this book you are well into the writing of your autobiography. If, by any chance, you haven't started, I urge you to begin immediately, before you lay the book aside and turn your attention to something else. You have an important contribution to make through your writing.

George Rochberg, a composer, famous for both his contemporary and traditional compositions, was once asked how he could maintain an equally intense interest in both modern and traditional music. His answer was, "If you don't let the traditions of the past feed you, you will die of malnutrition."

I don't say Americans are dying of malnutrition, but I do believe that as a society we are emotionally undernourished in terms of understanding and feeling a kinship with our heritage. Ours has been a society on a headlong dash into the future. Consequently, unlike many older cultures which have been built on generations of traditions we have, to some extent, misplaced our past.

Historians are writing about our confrontations with the former Soviet Union, about the making of presidents, about normalizing relations with China, but these things don't constitute our heritage. Our heritage is to be found in the day-to-day lives of those Americans, particularly members of our own family, who have gone before us.

You have the special privilege of providing a link to that heritage for future generations. Write about yesterday. Write about today, which will be history tomorrow. Continue to write about all of your todays until the very end of your life. Put the words on paper which will prevent your life and the lives of other members of your family from slipping into oblivion, leaving yet another generation of Americans with only a tenuous link to its heritage.

Good luck with your writing—have fun with it.

Assignments

Birth

Toys, first memories, and so forth

Parents, grandparents, and great grandparents

Brothers and sisters

Other relatives such as aunts, uncles, nieces, nephews, cousins, and more

Schools attended including elementary, high school, college, or other

Holidays

Birthdays

Failure and hope

Illnesses and remedies

Religion

Property you or your family have owned

How you survived the depression (if applicable)

Your children (if applicable)

Jobs

Politics: the civil rights movement, party politics, the women's movement, demonstrations in which you have participated, and more

Influence of wars on your life

Influence of music, theater, dance, movies, books, and painting on your life

Turning points in your life

Inventions

Hobbies

Marriage (if applicable)

Pets and other animals

Where were you on important days in history such as World War I Armistice Day, Pearl Harbor Day, D day, V-J day, V-E day, the day President Kennedy was shot, and more

Accomplishment of which you are most proud

Fashions

Family feuds (if applicable)

Games and sports

Talents

Famous people you have met

Different types of love such as romantic love, love for relatives or friends, and more

Have you grown in spirit?

Persons who have been a special influence in your life

Family traditions

Gifts—special gifts you have given or received

Special moments

Children and the things they say

Your special page (or pages)

Food

Your life today

Your plans for the future

Your attitude toward death

Courtship

Brief encounters

Immigrants

Brushes with physical danger

Unforgettable people you have met

Lessons you have learned

Natural disasters—blizzards, cyclones, earthquakes, floods, and more

Tears you have shed

Vacations and other trips

How you learned to do something new such as drive a car, ride a
  bike, or use a computer

Suggested Autobiographies

The following books represent only a small fraction of the thousand of autobiographies available at your library and in bookstores. Try some of these and make up your own reading list as well.

You might want to read an autobiography by someone who shares your interests. For example, if you like sailing, I'm sure you'll find something written by or about sailors (both professional and hobby sailors). The same will be true if you like art, politics, sports, or theater. Remember, too, that biographies are just as good as autobiographies for bringing up memories. They aren't quite as good in the sense of suggesting a style or format to you as autobiographies, but if you are only looking for a memory jogger, they will work very well. Just ask your librarian for help in finding the category you want. Remember, your librarian *wants* to help you, so don't be shy.

All in A Lifetime Frank Buck

An Autobiography Agatha Christie

At the Still Point Carol Buckley

The Autobiography of William Allen White William Allen White

Anne Frank: The Diary of A Young Girl Anne Frank

Anything Can Happen George Papashvily

Beyond Ourselves Catherine Marshall

Blue Highways William Least Heat Moon

Captain's Bride, General's Lady Maurine Clark

Dame of Sark Sibyl Hathaway

Drawn from Life Ernest Shepard

The Egg and I Betty McDonald

Family Circle Cornelia Otis Skinner

Family Gathering Kathleen Norris

The Gift Horse Hildegard Knef

Grandma Moses: My Life's Story Anna Mary Moses

Green Grows the Ivy Ivy Priest

Growing Up Russell Baker

The Heart Is the Teacher Covello Land

The Hiding Place Corrie Ten Boom

I Always Wanted To Be Somebody Althea Gibson

I Have Known Many Worlds Roger Burlingame

I Remember It Well Maurice Chevalier

Iacocca Lee Iacocca

I'll Always Have Paris Art Buchwald

It's Good To Be Alive Roy Campanella

A Joyful Noise Janet Gillespie

Kangaroos in My Kitchen Lorrain D'Essen

Land Below the Wind Agnes Newton Keith

The Life of a Salesman Marc Van Buskirk

Life Was Simpler Then Louis Erdman

Little Britches Ralph Moody

The Little Kingdom Hughie Call

A Little Learning Evelyn Waugh

Living by Faith Faith Baldwin

Lonesome Traveler Jack Kerouac

Looking Back with a Smile (A compilation of 100 stories from the Rocky Mountain Writers Guild's Senior Writing Competition). For information write: Senior Writing Competition; 7040 East Girard, Unit 303; Denver, Colorado 80224.

Merry Widow Grace Nies Fletcher

Minding Our Own Business Charlotte Paul

My Arabian Days and Nights Eleanor Calvery

My Autobiography Charles Chaplin

My Life with Martin Luther King, Jr. Coretta Scott King

My Lord, What A Morning Marian Anderson

Myself Among Others Ruth Gordon

The Nightmare Years, 1930-1940 William L. Shirer

On My Own Eleanor Roosevelt

On Reflection Helen Hayes

One Writer's Beginnings Eudora Welty

Only When I Laugh Gladys Workman

Our Hearts Were Young and Gay Cornelia Otis Skinner

Our Virgin Island Robb White

Outrageous Good Fortune Michael Burke

Portrait of Self Margaret Bourke White

Seven Winters and Afterthoughts Elizabeth Bowen

Shaking the Nickel Ralph Moody

Story of My Life Helen Keller

Testament of Experience Vera Brittain

Testament of Youth Vera Brittain

To Me It's Wonderful Ethel Waters

To Remember Forever Gladys Hasty Carroll

Travels with Charlie John Steinbeck

Twentieth Century Journey, 1904-1930 William L. Shirer

We Charles Lindberg

White Road, A Russian Odyssey, 1919-1923 Olga Ilyin

Acknowledgments

I wish to thank the following students, friends, and colleagues who have allowed me to reproduce their personal stories in this book: Dwynn Braun, Blanche Carstenson, Cecil Carstenson, Daisy E. Cavallero, Lydia Davidson, Robert Dempsy, Richard Dirks, Lorraine Elder, Romer Field, Lillian Flanders, Chester Garthwaite, Jan Goble, Mary Beth Gordon, Martha Hatfield, Patricia Jameson, Reginald Jeffro, Edith Johnson, Irene Kahn, Mary Mario, Elizabeth Martin, Ella Mather, Carol Nelson, Esther Nelson, Doris Pettit, Martha Rada, James Reed, Nancy Robb, Dora Scott, Jeanne Simmons, Helen Savage, Martin Schaefer, Margaret Sokoloff, and Robert Wills. I am also grateful to Professor William Hayashi of Central YMCA Community College, Chicago, for his assistance.

Aleon DeVore, contest coordinator for the Rocky Mountain Writers Guild's Senior Writing Competition, was especially helpful in the preparation of the second edition of *How To Write Your Own Life Story*. I am indebted to her for allowing me to include the writings of the following contestants from the Senior Writing Competition: Ethel

H. Allen, Norman W. Armbruster, Joseph Cohen, Earl Elezar Harris, Frank R. Martin, Betty Swords, John J. Toscano, and Edith Williamson. An asterisk follows each story written by a contestant from this competition.